C000180659

'This is powerful stuff from Paul E
example for leadership and pione
wonderful insights from this old E   ... on that has
essentially been exiled. His writing is really well crafted with lovely
turns of phrase and it's a book that is both a fairly easy read but also
runs deep. I found it inspiring and challenging in equal measure.'
Jonny Baker, Director of Mission Education, CMS

'By creatively using metaphors of exile and home, along with
insights from Ezekiel, Paul explores how exile can encourage our
imaginations to rethink and retool what church might look like.
I found this book to be challenging and hopeful for the place of the
church in our world, encouraging a humble and decentred posture
that might just make church more attractive to a generation that
craves authenticity and integrity.'
Cathy Ross, Lecturer in Contextual Theology, Ripon College Cuddesdon and
MA Coordinator for Pioneer Leadership Training at Church Mission Society

'*Home by Another Route* uses the metaphor of exile to describe
the place of the 21st-century church in a post Christendom
world. It argues that a new ecclesial narrative can be found by
understanding who we were, the acceptance of what we have
lost and through this the discovery of who we might be. This book
offers a valuable framework for those seeking to pioneer a future
expression of church.'
Ed Olsworth-Peters,National Officer for Pioneer Development, Church of England

'Worth reading for the first chapter alone! For non-experts, a great
introduction to the Old Testament exile and its acute relevance
today, especially for a church struggling to reimagine its missional
role in the contemporary world.'
Michael Moynagh, author and theological consultant to Fresh Expressions

The Bible Reading Fellowship
15 The Chambers, Vineyard
Abingdon OX14 3FE
brf.org.uk

The Bible Reading Fellowship (BRF) is a Registered Charity (233280)

ISBN 978 0 85746 631 0
First published 2019
10 9 8 7 6 5 4 3 2 1 0
All rights reserved

Acknowledgements
Unless otherwise acknowledged, scripture quotations are from The Holy Bible, New
International Version copyright © 1979, 1984, 2011 by Biblica. Used by permission.
All rights reserved worldwide. 'NIV' is a registered trademark of Biblica.

Extracts from the Authorised Version of the Bible (The King James Bible), the rights
in which are vested in the Crown, are reproduced by permission of the Crown's
Patentee, Cambridge University Press.

p. 84: Extract from 'Journey of the Magi' by T.S. Eliot in *Collected Poems 1909–1962*
(Faber and Faber Ltd, 2017). Used by permission.

Every effort has been made to trace and contact copyright owners for material used
in this resource. We apologise for any inadvertent omissions or errors, and would
ask those concerned to contact us so that full acknowledgement can be made in
the future.

A catalogue record for this book is available from the British Library

Printed and bound by Clays Ltd, Elcograf S.p.A

Paul Bradbury

HOME BY ANOTHER ROUTE

Reimagining today's church

For Emily

Contents

Acknowledgements

I had no great urge to write a book on the church or on Ezekiel until Mike Parsons invited me to consider the prophecy of the valley of dry bones as a text to explore. Out of that emerged the topic of exile and the renewal of the church. I am so grateful to Mike for the invitation and his encouragement to keep going when I felt unworthy of the task. Thanks too to my editor, Rachel Tranter, and the staff at BRF for shepherding me through the editing process with efficiency and understanding.

Thanks to the pioneer mission team at Church Mission Society, which I joined just as this book was beginning to form. Thanks to them and to Paul Burden at Sarum College, Salisbury for creating opportunities to try out some of this material. Jonny Baker and Cathy Ross kindly read the manuscript and helped develop it in the final stages, for which I am very grateful.

Peter and Fiona Hudd were immensely generous in the gift of their beautiful home as a space in which to write uninterrupted as the deadline loomed, even more so when the 'beast from the east' struck and left me snowed in for a day longer than planned!

Finally, my thanks as ever to my wife, Emily, for her affirmation of my writing vocation and encouragement to say what it felt needed to be said, and to my children Jacob and Bethany who by their presence constantly affirm the real value of returning home.

Introduction: 'Crisis? What crisis?'

Not far from where I live, on Dorset's Jurassic coast, is the village and bay of Kimmeridge. Overlooking the bay is Clavell Tower, a striking eleven-metre-high building, which sits close to the edge of the dramatic cliff that forms one side of the entrance to the bay. Clavell Tower has had an interesting life. Built by the local vicar as an observatory and folly in 1830, it was later used as a lookout by the coastguard until the 1930s. Having been gutted by fire, it stood unattended for years, its desolate appearance and location the inspiration for a crime novel, *The Black Tower* by P.D. James, in 1975. More recently, however, its fortunes have improved. Threatened by accelerated erosion of the cliff on which it stands, the decision was made to move the entire tower inland. The tower was dismantled piece by piece, each of its nearly 16,000 stones was numbered and catalogued, and then the whole thing reconstructed and renovated 25 metres away from the cliff. The tower's previous position is now remembered by a ring of foundation stones close to the encroaching cliff edge.

Clavell Tower is quite a feat of restoration. Returning the tower to its former glory, and raising the money for the work and materials, was one thing. But responding to the imminent crisis created by the power of the sea was another challenge entirely. It is a testimony to the value and importance we place on these historic buildings and landmarks that those involved had the vision and commitment to save such a beautiful building.

Yet – you can't help wondering how many years 25 metres amounts to. There are large, global forces at work here. The cliff continues to crumble at an alarming rate; at times, whole slices, a metre deep or more, disappear during winter storms. The coast path in the area requires rerouting in various places to respond to the landslides that are occurring now with regularity. Clavell Tower may have been restored to its former glory, but the crisis has not been averted. As things stand, Clavell Tower has simply been given a stay of execution. There is no more cliff to play with. One day, the tower and all its 16,000 stones will fall into the sea.

The church in the west faces a crisis, one created by a force of increasing intensity, unleashed in the deep sea of the Enlightenment era, whose eroding forces are at work at the very foundation on which the church as we know it stands. We touch on the reality of this crisis with talk of church renewal, church reform, church growth, of which there is much debate, much advice, much time and money invested. Yet how much of this effort ignores, consciously or not, the deeper forces at work at the bottom of the cliff we find ourselves on? How much of our attention is spent on restoring the building at all costs, without fully embracing the true reality of the environment in which that project is taking place? And how much of the effort involved under these headlines is made in the cause of simply moving the church inland, restoring the historic structure of the building away from danger and giving it a new lease of life. Crisis? What crisis?

Crisis is the very real and unavoidable context of the exile and the literature inspired by it. Israel's life had been destroyed, its structures and symbols literally burned by fire and its elite exported miles across the desert to Babylon. The Babylonian empire was now the pre-eminent force in the Near-Eastern world. It had been unleashing its power on the surrounding empires for decades, eating up territory, getting inevitably closer. It was surely only a matter of time until Jerusalem fell.

Yet, as the Babylonians withdrew from the charred wreck of Jerusalem, taking the ruling figures with them and leaving the poor to work the land under an appointed administrator, there were those who believed that all could be restored. There was a way back. The stones of Jerusalem could be numbered and catalogued and, one day, they would return and all would be back to the way things were. Crisis? What crisis?

One of the exilic writers in particular experienced almost all the horror of the exile first-hand. He grew up in Jerusalem and was a resident there when the first wave of exiles was taken to Babylon. He travelled as a captive across the desert to Babylon and, with his fellow exiles, began to learn how to live as an exiled people, while at the same time wondering what had happened to their home and whether they would ever see it again. That writer and prophet was Ezekiel. Among the vivid visions and prophetic actions of the book of Ezekiel is that of the valley of dry bones. The hand of the Lord takes Ezekiel and presents him with a vision of utter hopelessness and death. There is a valley 'full of bones' in which the Spirit leads Ezekiel 'back and forth among them' as though confronting him with the unyielding detail of his own despair. Having confronted Ezekiel with the pain and reality of the crisis of the exile, the Spirit asks Ezekiel a key question: 'Son of man, can these bones live?'

That question appears to have a simple answer, for the ground beneath the valley of dry bones is the ground of a foreign power. It is the ground of a foreign empire, one that worships foreign gods and one that has triumphed over the God of Israel. Ezekiel lived and exercised his ministry through the anticipation and realisation of the catastrophe of the fall of Jerusalem. What Ezekiel saw in the vision of the dry bones is what he had experienced: a stark and potent vision of the reality of exile, an exile that was viewed as utter death and destruction to all that seemed to Israel as fundamental to its identity and purpose.

For the western church, the ground beneath our feet has shifted. We describe this movement in a variety of ways: post-modern, post-Christendom, post-Christian. And in these descriptions, we point to the seismic nature of the movement we experience. Something fundamental is taking place and has taken place. Old landmarks, symbols and structures that could once be used reliably to orient our lives, our institutions, our faith, seem to have shifted or gone altogether. In this sense, we experience what Ezekiel and the captives in Babylon experienced; we experience exile.

Metaphors are a way of interpreting and reflecting on our own story and situation by laying alongside it the images and stories of another. The world of the metaphor connects at different points with the world we experience. We see connections and illuminations, as well as differences and mismatches. The more connections, the better the metaphor. Yet all metaphors have limitations. They cannot fully describe our reality, but they can help us understand it and respond to it more confidently.

I believe exile is a powerful metaphor for the church, particularly the western church, and perhaps even more particularly the church in the UK. We have not suffered the geographical dislocation that was the experience of the Babylonian captives, or which is the painful experience of many political dissidents or asylum seekers. So, while we must recognise the dangers of associating too closely with the emotions of exile, nevertheless we may well connect with a 'sense of the loss of a structured, reliable "world" where treasured symbols of meaning are mocked and dismissed'.[1] Others have explored the richness of this metaphor and argued its merits and deficiencies. That is not the main aim of this book. But a summary of our own experience of exile might be offered under two broad headings: disestablishment and decentring.

Disestablishment, though not yet a constitutional reality in the UK, is nevertheless a description of an ongoing process whereby the Christian church is increasingly losing power and influence in society. Remnants of another era still remain – civic churches, the Lord Spiritual, families coming for baptism, a chaplain to the Houses of Parliament, prayers at the start of local council meetings –

but these are remnants, often under threat or in decline. They are vestiges of the once-great edifice of Christendom, the constituted marriage between church and state which provided a place at the high table of power and influence for the church from Constantine in the fourth century onwards.

Christianity was the shaping story, the lingua franca, the DNA of social, cultural and political life for centuries. Now, it seems like an obscure myth in an old language that no one speaks any more. Many commentators and scholars will point to the Enlightenment and the philosophy of René Descartes, John Locke, Rousseau and others in the 17th century as opening the door to a fundamental undermining of the whole Christendom monolith. This 'age of reason' challenged the assumptions of Christendom at its very core with its assertion that knowledge can only be reliably attained by the reasoning individual. As this assertion worked its way into every area of life, the power and influence of the church as the arbiter of truth was subsequently diminished. Religion, not just Christianity, has been constantly re-evaluated since and seen its stock devalued. It has been told to retreat into the private sphere and stay out of public life. Its long and inauspicious association with political power and cultural hegemony has left it with a reputation it struggles to overcome. Consequently, religion in general, and the Christian church in particular, 'must now function within a framework that precludes any kind of cultural authority'.[2]

Decentring is a word that more describes the consequences of disestablishment. At one time, the church and the Christian faith it represented could count on a recognition and reputation within the life of western societies that made it central to people's lives whether they were believers or not. This is clearly no longer the case. Furthermore, it is precisely its perceived abuse of its position of power and authority, as part of the establishment, that puts it in a poor position now to provide any influence or make its voice heard. In that sense, many would say that the church is a church on the edge. That may well be our experience.

But while the church has been pushed from the centre, society has also lost any real sense of having a centre at all. It is not as straightforward as to say that the church has been thrust from the centre of cultural life and replaced with something else. In such a scenario, at least the church could come to terms with its new position and begin to reorient itself. Instead, there is no centre any more, or at least no communally agreed centre around which spiritual, cultural and political life can be oriented. Instead, 'culture is now an organised diversity with little sense of a defining centre'.[3]

In this context, the search for new models, new paradigms in which to organise and plan might well be futile. These sorts of approaches reckon on the emergence of a new status quo, a new kind of place, a new set of established relationships which remain dependable and predictable. But the nature of our new context is one of continuous change. In fact, perhaps the one predictable thing we experience is change itself.

So how might the church go about even asking the questions of its place and identity in this bewildering, challenging, disorienting context? The very unpredictability of the world we now inhabit mitigates against the standard methods of analysis. We cannot see our evolving context as a new system to analyse and understand so that we can put it together again in our minds and work out our place within it. There is no system. There is no place. Exploring who we are, and how we are to be in this new world, will require a very different mode of reflection.

Narrative resources offer us such an alternative mode of thinking. Sociologists now speak of 'flows' of images, data and capital as a way of making sense of culture and of describing cultural change. Culture is no longer static and definable, but its constant change is a layering of narratives within an environment of 'flows'. These flows are influences, pressures, incentives that shape and develop the stories of our lives and the lives of those around us. And so, when we are asked about ourselves, we invariably tell a story. We are telling our own particular narrative of identity within the multiple, layered narratives of those we live among. Of course, there are groups of narratives, networks of narratives, many ways in which narratives connect with one another. Where there is significant commonality, we might call this a culture. But even as we have placed the finger of definition on a story, the story starts to move on. Stories allow for change, for flow. They are, by their nature, averse to formulaism.

Perhaps, then, the most fruitful way to explore our place as the church in the maelstrom of our world is to play with story. What are the stories that connect best with the story we find ourselves in? A story is not like a map or a model. It will not lay itself over our half-formed version of events and tell us how things are, how things will be and therefore what we should do about it. But a good story will lie alongside the emerging story we find ourselves in and will act rather like a spiritual director. It will ask good questions, perhaps difficult questions. It will listen, probe, offer insight. It will gently but insistently force us to listen to ourselves, mine the truth from within ourselves and help move our story on. That is what I intend to try and do with the story of the exile.

The exile is, of course, a big story, told in numerous ways from various perspectives in the Bible. So, to make the task more manageable, I am using the vignette of Ezekiel's vision in the valley of dry bones as a window on the whole story. Ezekiel 37:1–14 is a concentrated image of exile, a story within a story, a prophetically symbolic acting-out of the story that has been and the *story that will unfold*.

That latter element makes it particularly rich for us. For not only does it detail the reality of exile, but it provides the hope of continuity and the trajectory of the future. And that future, in this vision and in other places in the exilic literature, employs another metaphor: the metaphor of home, or perhaps more accurately *homecoming*. 'I will settle you in your own land' (v. 14), says the Lord at the conclusion of the vision. There will be a homecoming; that is the promise.

Homecoming therefore provides a key connecting point in the overlaying of the world of exile with the world of our own crisis as the church in the secular west. Homecoming is there among the language of renewal and reform, in the literature and conference addresses on church growth. We may dress it up all we want, but really, as a church, we long for home in one way or another. We hope for an end to the disorienting experience of uncertainty and alienation in our own culture and search for a new kind of stability of identity and significance that feels like home. To start out on that journey may well be to glance over our shoulder to some vision of a remembered or imagined past, or it may be to venture boldly towards a vision of the future. Either way, it is a journey inspired by some concept of what it means for the church to come home.

However, as the title of this book implies, the kind of homecoming Israel may well have expected was not the kind of homecoming that transpired – and it was not, I believe, the kind of homecoming envisioned by God in the valley of dry bones. Exile was a point of departure for Israel in more ways than one, for it invoked a period of enormous creativity and reimagination in their communal life as the people of God. Israel did not simply number the stones of Jerusalem, return them on the basis of an established plan and rebuild. They did not simply return to the old ways with the crisis horizon moved far enough away for normal service to resume for a period of time. What Israel was invited to explore through the exile was more than restoration, or even reform and renewal – what they were invited to journey in was resurrection. Homecoming was promised, but in a way they could never have imagined or planned. This was homecoming, but by another route.

1

Exile: a story for our times

On Reading station

I was recently at Reading station with a few spare minutes and found myself standing next to a memorial plaque on the wall. The memorial is to a Henry West who, it says, 'lost his life to a whirlwind at the Great Western Railway Station, Reading, on 24 March 1840'. The final words of the memorial, a poem, refer to poor Henry West's quick and untimely death and then conclude thus:

Yet hushed be all complaint,
'tis sweet, 'tis blest,
to change Earth's stormy scenes
for endless rest.
Dear friends prepare,
take warning by my fall,
so you shall hear with joy
your Saviour's call.

This insight into 19th-century life, hidden in a quiet corner of a busy and modernised station that bears little if any resemblance to that within which the unfortunate Henry West lost his life, struck me as a poignant symbol of so much that has changed in the spiritual landscape of Britain since the whirlwind of 1840. It cannot possibly be said that the whirlwind-like events of our own era, which take too many lives with similar suddenness, could receive such a certain and hopeful response and in such a public form.

The Reading station memorial's words of comfort, warning and salvation remind us of a very different world where the language and assumptions of the Christian faith could confidently be recalled in the face of public tragedy. That world has surely been lost. The church may still be called upon to respond to tragedy. That was the case that same week I stood by the Reading station memorial in the aftermath of a terrorist attack in Manchester, only a few days before another terrorist attack in London and a few more before the Grenfell Tower fire in north Kensington. But it responds from a very different position. The Bishop of Manchester, who was a key figure in the city of Manchester's response to the terrorist attack there, later described his role as 'curating' the space in which people of many faiths and none could grieve and come to terms with what had happened in their city. One could only imagine what the response might be if a church leader had repeated the words for Henry West on such an occasion.

Standing next to Henry West's memorial, as the world hurried past on its urgent business, was a moment where I was struck by the force of change that has taken place in our country – and in particular by the sense of disconnection between a picture of the world painted by those words and the world I inhabit. I keenly felt my own disconnect, my own disorientation in a world that holds few if any of the certainties and convictions that enabled the Christian community to speak so plainly about faith and salvation. In such a world, there is no consensus about the narrative that shapes our response to tragedy and death. I felt alienated. I understood and appreciated the language of the memorial even while I recognised how it jarred with the world around me. The poem spoke to me of a world I connect with personally, yet a world that in any communal sense has utterly disappeared. For an instant, I felt the force of what it is to be an exile.

Israel's story of exile

The story of Israel's exile is well documented in the historical books of the Old Testament. There also emerges, around the historical record, a host of literature that reflects and wrestles with the experience and impact of what had happened.

The seeds of exile are sown when the kingdom of David and Solomon falls apart following the succession of Rehoboam to the throne. Jeroboam leads a rebellion which leads to the division of the kingdom into the northern kingdom of Israel and southern Judah (1 Kings 12).

Jeroboam's behaviour becomes a watchword for subsequent kings of the northern kingdom of Israel. Many of the kings of Israel that follow are judged by the history writers to have 'followed the ways of Jeroboam' (1 Kings 15:34; 16:19; 22:52), as though his act of intrigue and rebellion set the tone for the future of the breakaway kingdom.

A geopolitical reading of the story sees a small and vulnerable kingdom weakened significantly by the division into two. The two nations sit at a strategic location between a number of larger opposing empires whose own dominance rises and falls. There is Egypt to the south, Assyria to the north and, later, a resurgent Babylon to the east. The land of Israel is fertile and of strategic significance to all of them and it is not long before the two states become party to the attentions of these superpowers.

Fortunes fluctuate for northern Israel until the land is exiled by the Assyrians in 722BC, at the end of the reign of Hoshea. Israel by then is betting one superpower against another in terms of which can provide it protection. It is officially a protectorate of Assyria but Hoshea decides to defect to Egypt, with disastrous consequences (2 Kings 17:3–6). The population is deported to Assyria and the land repopulated with people from outside Israel (2 Kings 17:24).

Assyria then turns its attention to the southern kingdom of Judah. Sennacherib lays siege to Jerusalem but the city is delivered. However, a new power is emerging and starting to gain influence. King Hezekiah receives envoys from Babylon and shows them the riches of the palace vaults. He seems to think their visit trivial, brushing them off as people 'from a distant land' (2 Kings 20:12–14). But Babylon swiftly emerges as the dominant power in the region. The battle of Megiddo appeared to have established Egypt over its rival Assyria as the superpower of the region, with Judah paying it tribute. But Babylon invades Judah with such force that the Egyptian threat comes to abrupt end (2 Kings 24:7).

While the story of exile is the story of both Israel and Judah, the significance of the story really resides in the fate of Judah; for it is Jerusalem that signifies and symbolises the identity and destiny of the people of God. The first exile of Judah in 597BC, following the surrender of King Jehoiachin, sees the king, his family, officials and staff exiled to Babylon and another king, Zedekiah, appointed in his stead. However, when Zedekiah rebels nine years later, the response is ruthless. The Babylonians, under the reign of Nebuchadnezzar, lay siege to Jerusalem in 587BC and then, when the city is eventually breached, it is set on fire. 'Every important building he burned down', the writer of Kings tells us (2 Kings 25:9), including the royal palace and the temple. The king is removed in shackles to Babylon with his eyes gouged out, having also witnessed the murder of his own sons (Jeremiah 52:10–11). Another puppet-king is put in his place. While 2 Kings appears to end on a note of cautious optimism with the arrival of a successor to Nebuchadnezzar, it cannot wipe out the depressing end to the book which says that 'all the people from the least to the greatest, together with the army officers, fled to Egypt for fear of the Babylonians' (2 Kings 25:26).

Trying to ascertain accurate figures for the number of people exiled is difficult. 2 Kings 24:14 gives a figure for the first exile event of 10,000 and also includes 7,000 fighting men and 1,000 artisans (2 Kings 24:16), thus making a figure of 18,000. Jeremiah gives a smaller figure of 4,600 for the total carried off to Babylon in three separate events (Jeremiah 52:28–30). Rationalising these disparate figures may well be done by assuming that the Jeremiah figures only refer to men; including their families as well could give a far larger figure. These passages also make it clear that it was the ruling, military and artisan classes that were taken into captivity in a clear attempt to emasculate Judah as a viable state. There were citizens of Judah left in Jerusalem and the surrounding villages, but they were poor peasants, left only so that the land could continue to be cultivated (2 Kings 25:12).

There is little disputing that this is what happened to the kingdoms of Israel and Judah. The Old Testament biblical records of the events of the period are substantial. The landscape of the gospels, 400 or so years later, is one shaped by these events. Northern Israel's earlier exile and the repopulation of the land (Samaria) with foreigners is the backstory to the enormous prejudice shown to Samaritans in stories such as the good Samaritan (Luke 10:25–37) and in the encounter between Jesus and the woman the well (John 4:4–26). While the temple had been rebuilt by the time of Jesus, Jerusalem and the land remained under the jurisdiction of a foreign pagan power and had been so since the exile. The post-exilic stories of Ezra and Nehemiah, the rebuilding of the walls, are stories of great hope, stories that rekindle confidence in the covenant between God and Israel. Yet the exile remains definitive and the sense of the loss of Jerusalem and all that it represents profound and persistent. From that point on, the hope of restoration is at the forefront of the consciousness of Israel. To all intents and purposes, the exile is ongoing when Jesus emerges on the scene and the messianic hope and expectancy that greets him is a clear symptom of that.

The experience of exile

But what did it mean to experience exile? The biblical accounts clearly describe a disaster of enormous proportions for the people of

Israel. The siege of the city in 587BC was so severe that famine ensued (Jeremiah 52:6). When the city's walls are breached and the city is set on fire, the destruction is brutal and the loss of life considerable. Jerusalem is reduced to rubble (Psalm 79:1) and bodies litter the streets, attracting vultures and other scavengers (Psalm 79:2).

The book of Lamentations gives similar insights into the experience of the destruction of the city. Before the breaching of the walls, it describes the famine that had taken hold, leaving people to search desperately for food (1:11, 19). Lamentations details the effects of hunger and malnutrition (2:12; 4:8) and of people resorting to cannibalism to survive (2:20; 4:10). The destruction of the city appears to be near total (2:2) with the fire having consumed everything (2:3). The walls of the city have been flattened (2:8) and all the gates broken and destroyed (2:9). The city was abandoned (1:1) and dead bodies lay unburied in the streets (2:21). Survivors of the destruction of Jerusalem flee into the desert where they are vulnerable to the violence of bandits (5:9) and rape (5:11). The picture that the exilic books – some historical (2 Chronicles, 2 Kings), others prophetic (Ezekiel, Jeremiah) and poetic (Lamentations, Psalms) – build is one of a brutalised and traumatised people whose experience of violence and death is the dark background to all exilic and post-exilic literature.

There is, however, a more recent body of opinion that would play down the experience of exile. The argument is based in part on the lack of evidence for ongoing suffering, slavery or persecution of either those left behind in Judea or those deported to Babylon. It also draws on a critical interpretation of writers such as that of Chronicles who seems to overplay the impact of the destruction of Jerusalem by describing the land as virtually empty (2 Chronicles 36:16–21). There is growing evidence, however, to suggest that those who continued to live in Jerusalem were experiencing great suffering and that there was large-scale destruction and depopulation of Judean villages in the area. Archaeological evidence now suggests that those living in Jerusalem lived as not much more than squatters and that this situation changed very little until the arrival of Nehemiah in 445BC.[4] Research data also suggests that 80 per cent of population centres were abandoned or destroyed in that period.[5] One summary of the evidence puts it thus: 'The Babylonian conquest clearly brought total destruction to Jerusalem and the Judean sites to the south of Jerusalem.'[6]

Meanwhile, the experience of those deported to Babylon seems straightforward enough. Psalm 137 seems to sum up the pain of the exiles, whose tearful lament is elicited by the mere memory of Jerusalem (v. 1). Their experience is of persecution and scorn, of ridicule at the hands of their captors (vv. 2–3). There are passages that paint a more settled and peaceful picture for the exiles. Jeremiah's letter (Jeremiah 29) suggests a community able to settle down, to live peacefully, to marry, have children and generally get on with life (compare Ezekiel 33:30–33). However, other historical sources suggest that among the tactics of conquering empires in the Near East of the time was the forced labour of deported populations. Undoubtedly, thousands of destitute and homeless refuges from a razed city would have been easy candidates for the large-scale projects required by a growing empire. Indeed, there is evidence for the building of a huge canal system around the time of the Babylonians' conquest of Judah. The exiles, at least those Ezekiel was with, were at Kabur, a large canal near the city of Nippur, lending evidence to the theory that they were used as free labour in this massive engineering task.[7] The language of exile is also frequently dramatic, for example of being 'devoured', 'thrown into confusion', 'swallowed', 'vomited out' (Jeremiah 51:34). Common metaphors employed across the genre of the exilic books to describe the ordeal are words like 'bond', 'fetter', 'imprisonment'.

So what do we conclude from this evidence, both biblical and archaeological? The testimony of exile given in the books of the Bible describe multiple series of events around the destruction of Jerusalem which were brutally violent and traumatic. They also describe an experience of exile which continues to be harsh and painful for those who lived through it. While some passages may well point to a normalisation of life under both Babylonian rule in Judea and Babylon itself, there is little that argues for anything other than a perilous existence that is a mix of slavery, persecution, distrust and marginalisation within the dominant culture of the Babylonian empire.

But why does this matter? It matters because the experience in which the book of Ezekiel and other exilic writing emerges is key to understanding a theology of exile which we might reflect on in our own times. 'Any modern "theology of exile" must carefully recall their context, as well as our own context, for any theological reflection on the biblical experience.'[8] The experience of exile is as fundamental an element of the narrative of God's people as is the exodus. It is not just mere metaphor for those who follow after. It is as though their experience is part of our experience, their trauma is a resource for us, their response is a testimony on which we can draw with respect and confidence. It matters to understand it as well as we can, so that we can enter not just the words of Ezekiel and those he spoke and wrote among, enter not just his mind, but also his heart and soul.

The response to exile

As individuals, we know that our stories define us: stories of our origins, of those good and dependable things that have made us what we are, where we were born, where we grew up, our education, our parents and other significant relationships during childhood, in particular. But invariably, those elements of our story that have been difficult, even tragic, also play a huge part in shaping who we are. They form a significant part of our narrative, shaping it fundamentally, colouring it indelibly.

So it is for exile. It is clear that the narrative of the people of God takes an enormous and radical turn with the experience of the exile and the new reality that it produced. Far from obliterating the people of God, or rendering their faith and story null and void, the Babylonian exile 'evoked the most brilliant literature and the most daring theological articulation in the Old Testament'.[9] A number of themes become most creatively developed in the story of Israel and its literature at this point as responses to the experience of exile.

Firstly, **an emotional response**. Lament is given significant expression. Chief among these expressions is the book of Lamentations which, in five powerful and unashamedly detailed poetic chapters, describes the reality and experience of the destruction of Jerusalem. It is honesty and public sadness that typify this literature. Israel as a people has not only experienced horror but recognises that part of the process of healthily responding to this horror is to detail it and express it.

Detailing and expressing are different. The historians certainly do not shirk on the more prosaic facts of the narrative detail. But it is poetry that Israel turns to, in order to give expression to the visceral pain of these events. Jerusalem is not simply deserted; she is a widow (Lamentations 1:1), a metaphor that weighs the emptiness of the city with the pain of death, grief and desolation. The city is set on fire but is a fire that was 'sent… down into my bones' (Lamentations 1:13), a description that points to the fundamental and personal impact of the loss of the city's key buildings.

The choice of poetry also serves another fundamental need in the aftermath of suffering: the need to slow down. The book of Jonah, which is almost certainly written after the exiles, is a tight and picaresque story of just 48 verses. Nevertheless, it has a chapter of poetry (Jonah 2) just at the point where Jonah's story takes him down into the darkness of the deep sea and the belly of the great fish. It is as if the writer, aware of an audience desperate to move on with the hectic prose of the story and the promise of a resolution of Jonah's predicament, is determined to find a way to slow things down enough to listen to Jonah's pain, a pain which of course is theirs as well.[10]

It is not just what is written but the way it is written that reinforces the critical importance of telling it like it is, resisting the urge to minimise and the temptation to move on. Four of the five poems of Lamentations are acrostic poems, each line of which takes us through, in order, the letters of the Hebrew alphabet. The form is a disciplined one that guards against abbreviation and ensures that suffering is not devalued. The poem is ensuring that we stop and truly take in what has happened, and when we have done it once, we can do it again and again, four times. This happened, says the poem, and we won't forget it or allow the force of its impact to be diminished.[11]

Secondly, **a social response**. The language of exile is the language of homelessness, expressed very often in familial terms as having been cut off, forgotten, forsaken, *orphaned* by God (Lamentations 5:3, 20). It is as though the family line has been broken and Israel cast adrift. The use of lists and genealogies, like those in Chronicles, is one response to this sense of loss of family identity, a discipline of continuity in the face of utter discontinuity. Studies of refugees have pointed out how the ability to reconstruct a grounded life of meaning in an alien culture is related to their ability to create an agreed story of how things *were*. 'The refugee's self-identity is anchored more to who she or he was than what she or he has become.'[12] What is clear is that Israel suffered a profound loss of identity that elicited a determined effort to tell their story as a way of reaffirming the common understanding of who they *were* in order to begin to affirm who they *are*.

Thirdly, **a theological response**. The loss of Jerusalem, the royal palace and, above all, the temple is catastrophic. These buildings for Israel are not simply utilitarian structures; they symbolise and signify the faithfulness of a God who has entered into an everlasting covenant with one people: them. Their loss puts the fidelity of the covenant promise into complete disarray. Suddenly, the literature is replete with stories of a wholly different nature: doubtful, questioning, ambiguous, shocking stories that have the temerity to question the fundamentals of the covenant. Is God truly faithful? Is God truly powerful? Is God truly present? A significant strand of the book of Ezekiel focuses these questions on the temple, with the shocking vision of the glory of God departing from the temple (Ezekiel 10), coupled with the extended and detailed vision of the new temple and the return of God's presence (Ezekiel 43). This daring theological literature is offering a way out of the obvious response of despair and towards creative responses that begin to see the nature of God as being capable of expression in new and faithful ways, even in the midst of hostile captivity. They do not provide easy answers. Rather, they delight in interrogating the assumptions on which the status quo was based and begin to offer options for a people who thought being carriers of God's presence and salvation could only happen in a certain way.

Finally, **an ethical response**. A consistent message from the prophets and historians is that the patience of God has finally come to an end and Israel's constant rebellion and idolatry has now brought about his judgement. Jerusalem and the surrounding towns of Judah have been destroyed 'because of the evil they have done' (Jeremiah 44:3). The exile is a direct consequence of Israel's rebellion and stubbornness in the face of numerous warnings of impending judgement (Isaiah 40:2b). Yet this clear arithmetical logic of Israel's sin and God's judgement is also questioned. The book of Job, which most scholars believe also to be a work of the post-exilic period, is clearly bringing into question the straightforward logic of judgement in proportion to sin.

Job experiences a devastating series of calamities which destroy a settled, prosperous existence of some status. He spends the rest of the book defending his innocence to all those who remain convinced of the logic of his guilt, whether he is aware of it or not. This is dangerous stuff, questioning the foundation stone of Jewish theodicy and ethics, so it needs to come up with some clear alternatives – except it doesn't. God responds to Job's insistence on taking his plea to the highest authority but, when he does so, all reason or logic seems to have been left behind. The 'answer' to Job's question of fault would appear to be an overwhelming theophany (Job 38—41) that doesn't provide any logical satisfaction but instead seems to put Job's question into the perspective of a great mystery (Job 42:3).

The book of Jonah also pokes fun at the sin/judgement basis of Jewish ethics. A single, short warning from Jonah in the city of Nineveh, a city with as horrific a reputation as Babylon for cruelty and ruthlessness, brings the Ninevites to repentance (Jonah 3). 'I knew that you are a gracious and compassionate God, slow to anger and abounding in love, a God who relents from sending calamity,' states Jonah angrily, in response to the deliverance of Nineveh (Jonah 4:2). But is this not an ironic statement placed alongside the consensus on the reasons for the exile? Jonah's audience recognises Jonah's doctrinal statement as their own and yet have to place it against the explanation for their own suffering which seems to be that of a God of judgement, not mercy. As seems so often the case with exilic literature, this paradox is not resolved. Rather, it serves as an invitation to play, wrestle, explore in a new kind of highly creative space beyond the old certainties of the past.

The metaphor of exile

Before we come to explore Ezekiel 37 itself, this chapter has taken some time to cover the ground of the events and impact of the exile on the people of God. This is the necessary groundwork of examining the nature of the story which will be used to engage critically with our own experience as custodians of the promises of God. Other stories can act as narrative partners for our own experience as the people of God in our own times. A colleague of mine would cast his vote for the exodus as the key shaping story for our age. Dr Sam Wells uses the story of David and Goliath to explore similar themes on the current state of the church. The story asks, who is the church? Is it David? Or Goliath? Wells argues:

The problem is that the church has assumed for as long as anyone can remember that it's supposed to be Goliath. It's supposed to be huge, it's supposed to be important, it's supposed to be a player on the national stage, it's supposed to be the acknowledged voice of the people. All the things Goliath was. All the things David wasn't.[13]

Immediately, the story helps us see things about our assumptions that we were perhaps not willing to see. It asks difficult questions of us that we would not ask of ourselves.

However, this is not about finding the best metaphor or a perfect match; each story, each metaphor provides valid and important insights and offers new perspectives for our own experience:

The usefulness of a metaphor for rereading our own context is that it is not claimed to be a one-to-one match to 'reality' as though the metaphor of 'exile' actually *describes* our situation. Rather, a metaphor proceeds by having an odd, playful and ill-fitting match to its reality, the purpose of which is to illuminate and evoke dimensions of reality which will otherwise go unnoticed and therefore unexperienced.[14]

The context is everything. The story of the exile places the people of God in a context which was unique and, for us, highly apt. They knew what it was to reach a sense of having fulfilled what it meant to be God's chosen people. The covenant promises appeared to have been fulfilled in the establishment of the kingdom of Israel under David and then Solomon. Surely this was what it meant to be the people of God? Surely this was the default setting for being God's chosen people? The language, symbols, rituals and rhythms of life associated with this time of the history of Israel seemed normative. The story is of the establishment of a kingdom under God's rule through the rule of an anointed king, and of the establishment of a system and structure for hosting and administering the holy and purifying presence of God. This seemed like the inevitable result and fulfilment of a process of development under God's provision and direction. And yet, in the course of a generation, all of this had disappeared.

We know that something similar is happening to us as God's people in the developed western world. 'As long as anyone can remember,' says Wells, we have assumed things about ourselves. And at times we have reverse-engineered theologies to suit that view of ourselves – much like Israel did. But now we must learn to think again, because in the course of a generation or two the assumption that forged, apparently for all eternity, a place for the church in the landscape for our culture, has all but disappeared.

That assumption, that structure, both physical and mental, of identity, status and practice is often called Christendom. It has formed the basis for our sense of place in our own culture for the past 1,500 or so years. The assumption made was that Christianity, as a set of beliefs and collection of practices, played a significant if not defining role in the shaping of our culture and in the day-to-day experience of life for everybody within the western nations. That assumption has now been eroded to the point of collapse over the last century. To read a longer narrative of the process of exile for the church, you might like to read: Phyllis Tickle, *The Great Emergence* (Baker Books, 2008); Michael Frost, *Exiles* (Baker Books, 2006); or Lee Beach, *The Church in Exile* (IVP, 2015). Each traces the shift the church has experienced, accelerating since World War II, from a place at the centre of things to an uncertain place as just one voice in the marketplace of ideas, one player in an evolving drama on a very crowded stage. As Brueggemann describes it:

There was a time... when the Christian preacher could count on the shared premises of the listening community, reflective of a large theological consensus. There was a time, when the assumption of God completely dominated western imagination, and the holy Catholic Church roughly uttered the shared consensus of all parties. That consensus was rough and perhaps not very healthy, but at least the preacher could work from it.[15]

Or, as Lee Beach puts it:

> In the post-Christian revolution, it is fair to say that the church is one of those former power brokers who once enjoyed a place of influence at the cultural table but has been chased away from its place of privilege and is now seeking to find where it belongs amid the ever-changing dynamics of contemporary culture.[16]

As with Israel, the initial forms of responses we may want to make to this predicament are perhaps denial and despair before they can ever become hope or creativity. If Israel's experience was one of homelessness, a metaphor which encompasses both the loss of core relationship as well as the elements of displacement and disorientation, then the desire to rediscover home could come through a nostalgic vision of restoration, assimilation into the dominant culture or, somehow, a creative reassertion of identity in the alien context.

If we too have been made homeless, 'chased away', to use Beach's term, from our sense of place within western culture, then we too are looking for routes home – and perhaps we can already begin to see, with the application of this metaphor, the extent to which we are in denial, despair or hope. We may be aware of the extent to which we are looking longingly over our shoulder to find a way home or looking into the uncertainty of the landscape in front of us. (That might even be seascape, for there is nothing certain about the surface in front of us, which is surely more fluid than solid.)

What becomes clear from the exilic literature, and increasingly from our understanding of the life of the exiles in both Babylon and Judea, is that a road beyond denial and despair began to be navigated. The two great temptations of despair and assimilation appear to have been worked through creatively, and beyond them a new way of being faithful to their call and identity as the people of God began to emerge. If we follow this story and reflect carefully on it for our own context, might we too begin to create new paths, new imaginations, new confidence in our own explorations of the way ahead?

2

Picking over the bones

The hand of the Lord was upon me, and he brought me out by the Spirit of the Lord and set me in the middle of a valley; it was full of bones. He led me back and forth among them, and I saw a great many bones on the floor of the valley, bones that were very dry.

EZEKIEL 37:1–2

Perhaps my most powerful experience of exile, in the sense of dislocation, was some years ago when our basement flat in London was flooded during a particularly powerful summer storm. The main drain, which ran down the main road on which we lived, was also a culverted river. When the storm hit, it couldn't cope with the sheer volume of water coming into it. A mixture of run-off and sewage came up through the toilets, down off the road and into the row of flats, all below ground level. Thankfully, we were not there at the time. A neighbour managed to get through to us to say that there was a long row of fire engines along our road and they were worried for us. We called a friend who had been charged with watering our garden. Thinking we were ringing to remind him, he started by saying it was okay because it had been raining quite a lot! We sent him down to take a look – he rang back and gave us the news that all that we owned was ruined, either because it had been underwater or because it was contaminated by raw sewage. People's possessions all along the street were being turfed out into a row of skips and disposed of.

We returned to London to lodge with friends and visited the flat to see the place for ourselves. By then, the flat had been emptied and the water gone. There was a dirty slick of a line all along the walls about three feet from the floor marking the extent of the flood. And that was pretty much it. The place was empty and bare. All our furniture, books, pictures, photos and artefacts were gone and the place echoed with the eerie noise of emptiness. Except, that is, for a few shards of broken blue glass, strewn in one corner of our bedroom. They were the remains of a bedside lamp. That was all that was left of everything we could remember owning: little pieces of dark-blue glass. I can recall their look and feel, even the sound of them under my feet, even now. They became a symbol of what happened that day while we were somewhere else, a symbol of the loss not just of our possessions, but of the home in which we had lived, which was now gone.

In a similar way, Ezekiel's journey into the valley and his Spirit-led tour of the dry bones is a return to the place of a dramatic loss of home. Ezekiel had experienced a part of this event, though not the traumatic siege and destruction of the city. He will have heard the stories and the first-hand experiences of those coming from Jerusalem in the second wave of exiles. He will have seen the pain and the loss on their faces, and heard much of the detail of what had happened. But he had not truly been confronted with the loss. But now, as the Spirit leads him in the valley, he is asked to engage with it up-close and confront its reality and its pain.

It seems entirely apt that this vision of Ezekiel should take place in a barren valley beyond the bounds of the city Babylon, where the beleaguered community of exiles lived. Ezekiel's life had become one of standing alone in the deserted space between one camp and another, one set of opinions and another. Yet his life had also brought him to a place that was peripheral, exiled not only from his homeland, but also from among the very people he was ministering to. This was not at all how his life had started out.

Ezekiel was born in Jerusalem to a priestly family. He had an establishment upbringing, and was educated and trained in preparation for a position within the institution of the priesthood at the centre of life in Judah. He was also born at a time of great hope and change. It was the year that the book of the law was rediscovered (2 Kings 22), an event which appears to have energised and encouraged the programme of reforms that King Josiah was making. It seemed, then, that Ezekiel's life was to be one of traditional priestly service within a renewed and reformed institution.

But political events changed all that. Josiah's death at the battle of Megiddo in 609BC brought his son Jehoahaz to the throne. His reign was short-lived. The Egyptians exiled him and imposed heavy taxes on Judah. Within three months, Pharaoh Necho had put his brother Jehoiakim in charge, allowing him to reign in Jerusalem as a vassal king. Then Babylon, having won the definitive battle of Carchemish in 605BC, gradually exerted their dominance over the whole region. They made Jehoiakim their puppet king and for three years Judah paid allegiance to them. Then Jehoiakim rebelled and the Babylonians invaded. The death of Jehoiakim brought his son Jehoiachin to the throne and within three months he had surrendered the city. It was at this point, in 597BC, that a 25-year-old trainee priest by the name of Ezekiel was deported, along with perhaps 10,000 other members of the nobility and the priestly, military and skilled classes of Judah to the distant city of Babylon.

It is worth dwelling for a moment on the expectations Ezekiel would have had for himself as a priest. The priesthood was hereditary and deeply established. Everything about Ezekiel's life up to this point was oriented towards this profession. It marked his identity; it shaped his mind, his heart and the rhythm of his days. It gave him identity, status, purpose and presence:

> His ministry as a priest would sustain the moral and spiritual fabric of the universe by preserving the essential distinctions inherent in all of life – the holy and profane, the clean and the unclean. He would sustain all this through the grand rituals of blood sacrifice, standing as a priest at the very fulcrum

of interaction between God and humanity. Above all, he would have intimate access to the place of Yahweh's eternal dwelling.[17]

So here is a man with a deep sense of the institutional fabric of his society and a profound assumption of what his status and role within that society would be. It is to individuals like Ezekiel that the exiles would surely have looked for guidance in the immediate aftermath of the deportation. Everything about their life had been torn apart and destroyed, all ways of being who they were no longer open to them. The temple was thousands of miles away. The sacrificial system and the assurance of the sustaining presence of God in their midst had been removed from them. They were people who felt as if their heart and soul had been removed from them and left behind. But Ezekiel was with them. And surely his job was to give them hope, as someone at the heart of the institution, that all will eventually be well, things would eventually return to normal. After all, Jerusalem could be rebuilt, and the remains of the temple could be restored. It was only a matter of time, surely, before the exiles could return and life go back to normality.

However, Ezekiel's vocation then takes a different direction. Having been exiled once with his people, Ezekiel is called to be a prophet (Ezekiel 2). And surely, through this profound experience, Ezekiel finds himself an exile among his own people, for the place of a prophet was utterly different from the place of a priest. You did not inherit the position of prophet. There was no Department of Prophecy in the religio-political structures of Jerusalem. Prophets were oddball wilderness characters, no doubt sought out for wisdom in times of crisis, but not people to be trusted and rarely people to keep close at the centre of things. They were too dangerous. To be a prophet was to position oneself at the edge, precisely in order to be able to see things as a critical outsider. So 'as a prophet [Ezekiel] was called to identify with the voices of those who dared to call in question this whole massive edifice of theology, and ritual'.[18] His call turned Ezekiel from an establishment figure to a dissident.

Scholars of Ezekiel recognise in his prophecies the legacy of his elder contemporary, Jeremiah. Jeremiah was prophesying in Jerusalem in the time of Josiah, Jehoiakim and Zedekiah, from the time of the reforms of Josiah through to the destruction of Jerusalem. Jeremiah was not exiled along with Ezekiel and wrote to the exiles from Jerusalem (Jeremiah 29). True to the prophet's calling, he was a thorn in the side of Jehoiakim and Zedekiah, in particular warning of the impending disaster, calling them to repentance and refuting the false prophets of the time who advised various futile alliances or outright military resistance. It was Jeremiah who prophesied the destruction of the temple during the reign of Jehoiakim, warning them that, unless the idolatry taking place in the temple was repented of, the temple would be destroyed and the city with it (Jeremiah 26). This heretical message brought Jeremiah the threat of death and turned him into a pariah in the eyes of the establishment. The idea that the temple, the holy place of God's presence, could be destroyed was anathema – would not God protect his own house, his own dwelling place? Had he not done this miraculously during the time of Hezekiah (2 Kings 19)?

Ezekiel was a teenager when Jeremiah was delivering his prophetic warning in Jerusalem. He would certainly have heard what was happening, the tenet of the message and the stir that it caused in the priestly profession and political classes. He therefore knows, standing 'among the exiles by the Kebar River' as the heavens are opened and the extraordinary vision that introduces his call as prophet unfolds, what the life of a prophet would likely involve. Any career prospects Ezekiel may have harboured, back in Jerusalem, were now gone. But, perhaps most painful – as an exile, already reeling from five years as a priest and alien among the pagan Babylonians, unable to carry out his ministry, searching for his identity – was the realisation that this call meant a kind of exile from the remnant of his own people, forging a counter-identity in the margins of Babylon.

Yet held within the dual calling in Ezekiel's life to both priesthood and prophet is the dynamic possibility of reformation and renewal.

Ezekiel, as priest, was a person centred on God. The priestly call was to draw people constantly, through the sacrificial system, to orient all of life around the presence of God. As a priest, he also understood the establishment, the structures, the foundational principles on which the life of Jewish society functioned. So, as a prophet, he knew precisely what he was critiquing; he knew exactly what his subsequent warning of future calamity meant. Yet his love for God, in this wildly different context, alongside his deep understanding of the institutions of the Jewish religion, brought him to a place where a new and faithful expression of life could begin to emerge.

In modern terms, we might call Ezekiel a pioneer minister. His call takes him to a place that most pioneers recognise: a place where a love for God and a love for his church, as an agency of his mission in the world, are in constant creative dialogue with a love for community and people on the edge: exiles. This is a place where the gospel and the traditions of the church require an imaginative but faithful engagement with culture. It requires a knowledge and familiarity with both, and the ability to make creative connections between the two.

But pioneers themselves often feel like exiles. Their call has invariably taken them to the margins of the structures. This can be a painful experience. Pioneers are easy to ignore, distrust, even malign. They do not fit. But for them, that is a gift, the 'gift of not fitting in'.[19] The perspectives of pioneers can be challenging, irritating and cast as irrelevant or heretical. But they are crucial perspectives.

The imaginative and creative responses of the exiles can surely only have emerged by the permission-giving leadership of prophetic leaders like Ezekiel who opened up a new kind of space: a space in which the answer to crisis did not have to be simply a return to the old ways, but rather it could be a space in which new solutions could take shape without the threat of censor. Brueggemann calls Ezekiel 'the subversive traditionalist', 'an imaginative practitioner of the root tradition of Israel'. 'He knows and affirms the tradition which is rooted in the oldest credo recitals, but he rereads the tradition in the light of his own incongruous situation.'[20]

Gerald Arbuckle calls pioneer leaders and people like Ezekiel 'dissenters'. We may hear that word negatively, but we would do well to listen to its creative potential:

> Dissenters reframe things we take for granted by offering new ways of viewing issues or putting them into contexts we did not previously think possible. Dissenters expand our imaginations. They are upside-down thinkers, terribly annoying to us when we are too attached to the security of our idea or habits, but very necessary if we want to know what God wills of us.[21]

Others call such innovators 'walk outs':[22] people with the courage and conviction to take themselves out of the dominant system in order to begin to create something new. Such people rarely come from nowhere; they generally come from within the system but there is something in their makeup and their story that brings them to the edge, the 'chaordic space'[23] where innovation and creativity can happen. Ezekiel is not exactly a 'walk out' in the sense that he has a great deal of choice in finding himself where he is. He has been called out to a community on a new frontier at the edge of their geography, the edge of their experience, the edge of their resistance – and then further out, to the edge of this community itself. He is truly a subversive, a dissident, a pioneer: an exile among the exiles.

'Back and forth among' the bones of death

The vision that Ezekiel receives is pivotal in the context of the whole book. There are four visions in the book, including the inaugural vision. Two of these take place on the plain outside the settlement where Ezekiel resides with the community of exiles. The first (3:22–27) results in Ezekiel acting out a prophetic symbol of what is to come: he will be bound with ropes, confined to his house, his tongue stuck to the roof of his mouth, unable to speak, unable to carry out his ministry of rebuking and warning of what is to come. It is as though Ezekiel becomes in his physical being a symbol of God's intention to bring about the consequences of his people's rebellion.

So, while the first vision on the plain beyond the Kebar River is a presage to destruction, the second vision is a promise and a vision of renewal and life. And yet, before this extraordinary vision of hope can begin to unfold, Ezekiel must walk among the dead. The Spirit 'led me back and forth among them, and I saw a great many bones on the floor of the valley, bones that were very dry' (37:2). This seems to me a profound piece of detail. You might be forgiven for thinking that the pure visual force of the valley 'full of bones' was enough to communicate a clear and powerful message to Ezekiel – a vision of death, destruction and hopelessness. Yet somehow that is not enough. The Spirit leads Ezekiel on a detailed tour of the valley, 'back and forth among them'.

This must surely have been a harrowing experience. Was it not enough to have lived among the exiles for so long? Was it not enough to have prophesied the destruction of Jerusalem and then witnessed the arrival of thousands more exiles from the destroyed city? To have heard their stories of death, starvation, brutality and murder? To have seen the visible testimony of the siege, the fire and the journey through the wilderness? Yet this is what the Spirit does to someone intimately acquainted with the realities of the death, grief and suffering of the exiles – he leads Ezekiel 'back and forth among them'.

Why? Firstly, because Ezekiel is not to be just a witness to the death of a nation; he must also personally identify with that death. Ezekiel is still a priest. As a Jewish priest, he had been trained in the disciplines of cleanliness. One such discipline is of keeping himself from physical contact with death. Any such contact renders him unclean and unfit to carry out his duties. As the Spirit leads him up and down through this valley of death, he is confronted with the effective death of his status and role as a priest. The temple has gone. Jerusalem has gone. All the established structures and artefacts that make the vocation and practice of priest possible lie burned and ruined in the dust of Jerusalem. Now any dreams or ambitions he may have ever had for his vocation, his career, are gone. Before the destruction of Jerusalem, he lost his voice, his ability to prophecy and resorted to symbolic drama to try and get his unpopular message across. Now he is no longer, effectively, a priest. Ezekiel is confronted with the loss of his own life, as the nation he represents loses its life.

Secondly, because the reality of the destruction of Jerusalem, and with it the destruction of any hope of a return to the kingdom of Judah as it was, must be conveyed emphatically. For generations, prophets and kings had colluded to offer hope of a return to some nostalgic vision of an established kingdom. That hope is now utterly dismissed. The scale of the scene is one thing, but the detail is another. That the bones are 'very dry' means they have been left out under the desert sun, left for vultures and wild animals to pick the flesh clean, left for the brutal sun to bleach and dry them. These are bodies left unburied for a considerable time. That they are unburied means they are under a curse. The defeat of this 'vast army' (37:10) is not just poor planning and naive strategy; God is at work in this. This death is a definitive reality, not a mere setback. 'In the end, it is God and not the Babylonians who terminated the temple project.'[24]

Lament and the possibility of hope

But, like the dark poetic chapter of Jonah and the acrostic poems of Lamentations, that little phrase 'back and forth among them' (37:2) signifies the profound need for the slow attention to pain, death, hopelessness and defeat. It signifies the Spirit's invitation to a spirituality of honesty, to a faith that won't look away or create false narratives of hope or triumph when the blatant reality of defeat lies at our feet in stark and vast horror.

Lament is the word we use for such attention to and voicing of pain. Biblical lament, however, is not just a kind of release or catharsis. Biblical lament is the gift of a shape or form for our pain and suffering. Lament provides a safe and legitimate container to bring us to our pain and our pain to God. Old Testament scholars now recognise a lament form in the psalms. Perhaps a third of the psalms are characterised as laments; a form or pattern for these psalms is evident. This form gives space for complaint and rage but also, as the psalm develops, for intercession and recommitment of our faith in a God who appears to have let us down. What is most telling in all the psalms of lament is that each one (with one exception) ends on a doxology of praise.[25] In other words, what is happening in lament is that the person of faith is being given a pattern within which to voice pain, confusion, doubt and loss. Yet it is also a pattern that leads to hope and ultimately to praise. Lament is God's gift to us to enable fierce and *faithful* honesty in the context of suffering. The complaint within lament is not a precursor to faith; *it is faith*. Without that commitment to honesty and 'telling it like it is', we jeopardise faith, putting ourselves at risk of despair or duplicity.

The tour of these bones is Ezekiel's form of lament. As he walks up and down among the dried-up remnant of a powerful army – up and down, back and forth – it is like the verses of a long poem, the repeated dirge of a funeral march, the slowly read list of the fallen at a war memorial. With each step, each traverse across the valley, Ezekiel is learning the particular language of lament for his generation, his people, at this time. He cannot preach hope unless he walks this journey of lament from one side of the valley to another, again and again, until he is exhausted, physically and emotionally. Four short words – 'back and forth among' – but they are shorthand for everything ever written about the truth of the exile, the siege, the fire, the staggering loss, the death walk through the desert and all its significance for the people of Israel.

Singing the Lord's song in a strange land

What does this move of the Spirit in the valley of dry bones have to say to our own generation? The language and imagery of death may seem hyperbolic for own experience; after all, we are not truly experiencing our own demise in the way this story portrays, are we? Perhaps not. However, the finality and irreversibility of what has happened to the position and status of the church in the west is significant. 'For the truth is that the old, settled advantage in the world upon which we have counted is over and gone, as over and gone as was Jerusalem's temple.'[26] For many, there is a grief and a loss, a disorientation and a bewilderment at how to 'sing the Lord's song a strange land' (Psalm 137:4, KJV) when such songs were only ever learned in a land that seemed to understand and appreciate them. While not everyone will necessarily feel pain at the displacement of the church in our culture, there does require in all of us a harsh and resolute honesty to the situation. We must work at being, as Brueggemann suggests, 'communities of honest sadness', communities that 'name the losses'.[27] The importance of this, as it was for Ezekiel, is in being faithful even in the face of loss, but also in providing a bulwark against complacency and denial of the reality of the situation we face:

> This community of sadness has as its work the countering of a 'culture of denial' which continues to imagine that it is as it was, even when our experience tells us otherwise.[28]

The truth is that every community will be a messy mixture of deniers and grievers, prophets and pioneers. It is for the visionaries like Ezekiel, the priest-prophets, to be leaders in hope to a community that will be a blend of despair, nostalgia, reality and unreality. Telling true stories of reality, no matter how painful, is part of being that kind of leader in hope. Such stories open up the possibility of a way forward – they acknowledge the pain and loss – but in doing so, make it possible for people to move on and begin to define an alternative reality. Consequently:

Defining reality is an act of empowerment, because it orients people in a way that allows them to proceed with the facts as they currently stand. Without this act of truth telling, a legitimate hope can never emerge.[29]

Bishop Graham Cray, when leader of the Fresh Expressions movement in the Church of England, used to tell one such powerful story of reality:

A woman walks into a church; we don't really know why, perhaps to find some cool on a hot day, perhaps because of some other motive. She is young and unaccustomed to being in church buildings. She wanders round the church, which… has a range of symbols and imagery depicting aspects of the story of the Christian faith. The vicar of the church happens to be in the building and begins to notice this young lady wandering quizzically round the church, clearly uncertain of what she is looking at. Eventually, he approaches the lady and asks if there is anything he can do to help. 'Thank you,' she says. 'I was just wondering what this building means, what it's all for.' Sensing an opportunity, and looking to engage this lady personally in some way, the vicar sees the crucifix the woman is wearing and says, 'Well, it's all about the person you've got hanging round your neck.' The woman looks down at her necklace and immediately says, 'Oh! I always wondered who the little man was!'[30]

I have heard gasps of almost horror when this story has been told: disbelief that someone could be so close to Christian culture and yet so utterly disconnected from it. But perhaps the real horror is that so many people find that story surprising. Much of the church is so protected from the reality of our own exile that this is in effect its own form of unconscious denial.

When I was a curate, I remember a lady I knew a little from the school run coming to church one Sunday. We were a struggling, elderly church, trying hard to make connections with parts of our community that were not represented by the congregation, so someone like her turning up was a moment of hope. I didn't manage to speak to her immediately after the service, but the next morning we ended up walking back from the school run together. 'I came to your church yesterday,' she said. 'I know. I saw you.' 'I won't be coming again.' 'Oh, why is that?' 'Because almost as soon as I got there, you told me I was a bad person.' And so she went on to explain how she felt once the first hymn had finished and we came to the confession. Rather than this experience being an opportunity for reflection and receiving forgiveness, she saw it as confirmation that uppermost in the minds of Christians was the need to remind people that they are bad and unworthy.

It is easy to dismiss these sorts of stories, perhaps as the normal kind of confused and ill-informed responses of people engaging with Christian language and symbolism. After all, isn't anything we do in church a bit weird to the outsider? However, I see them as precious stories that speak volumes about our place in the secular landscape in which we minister. These are stories we must listen to, for they speak a little of the truth of what is happening in our culture – we ignore them at our peril.

These stories also illustrate just how complex and bewildering the current cultural landscape is: a mixture of ignorance, alienation and confusion created by both secularism and the echoes of dominant religion. Exile is not straightforward. The language of Christendom continues to hold a powerful influence, so the reality of this cultural landscape must be faced – and faced truthfully. At times this is frustrating. Trying to communicate the heart of God's love for people into this milieu starts to feel as if we have travelled to a foreign country but brought the wrong phrasebook. At times this is painful, as we experience a dislocation and an alienation that we feel ill-prepared for or powerless to do much about.

On the other hand, there are also things that we tell ourselves in order to avoid walking back and forth among the bones. They are stories that sound hopeful but are not rooted in reality. Jerusalem, prior to its destruction, was not short of prophets willing to tell people what their fears desperately needed to hear. The biblical literature records the opposing narratives that were the focus of debate and conflict. Jeremiah, for example, records the prophecy of Hananiah, who weaves a story of unrealistic hope in the aftermath of the exile, a story born out of the familiar narrative of God as a mighty warrior who would triumph over the false gods in time (Jeremiah 28). This promise of a military turnaround and the eventual subjugation of Babylon to the power of Israel would have gone down well in Jerusalem. Yet Jeremiah rebuked him publicly, and was ultimately vindicated.

I heard a bishop tell another memorable story, one told precisely to bolster hope and confidence among a group of church leaders. He told of how he had been to a harvest festival in a village church somewhere in the depths of the countryside. The church was packed. And it was so full that, by his reckoning, there were more people in church that day than there were residents of the village.

This was a story of hope. Or was it a story of denial? What church's numbers aren't boosted by a visit from the bishop? And what village church, in a rural farming community, where the traditional rhythms of land and religion run deep, isn't busier than usual at harvest festival? And besides, when the only service for a cluster of small villages was in that church on that particular day, is it surprising that the congregation outnumbered the official population?

There are plenty of stories from church leaders that cast a very different vision of the health of the church, and which suggest that this story is not quite the hopeful vision the bishop and everyone else would like it to be. Granted, bishops get a particular perspective on church life as they go from one festival, confirmation, ordination, patronal saint's day to another. Perhaps they can be forgiven for a rather hagiographic image of the church they lead. Yet they must surely be led 'back and forth among' the bones from time to time by leaders or other members of the Christian community who have found the courage to tell their own perspective on the truth. If we need our leaders to do anything at this time of uncertainty and disorientation, it is unflinchingly to tell the truth of our situation, whether that is popular or not.

This is where the story of exile itself, as a way of distilling a truthful narrative from the competing narratives of our day, can have a powerful truth-telling effect. In my own ministry, I have worked with leadership teams of emerging fresh expressions of church, offering a coaching-based approach to training as they explore new ways of being church for their own context.[31] One team had set up a new informal and all-age service in their village hall. The team was mixed. Some went to an earlier, more traditional service in the village church but saw the new community as a source of hope for the future, so supported it. Despite this support for the emerging community, the hearts of one or two were still for the renewal of the traditional congregation. 'If we just do the traditional stuff really, really well, people will come!' one of them said. Others clearly saw the fresh expression as their community and had little hope for the more traditional service reaching the younger families that they represented. This produced a vibrant conversation among the team, as some fought for the ongoing viability of the traditional congregation while others saw the future in the new.

Things began to clear, however, when we explored the story of exile. Not that I used the language of exile – but when we told the story of the cultural transformation of the UK and its impact on traditional motifs of church life – Sunday, baptisms, weddings, funerals, biblical literacy, familiarity with the environment of the church, the image of the clergy – something began to change. For one man in the group, in the course of an evening, there was a shift from belligerent support for the traditional done well, to a recognition that it was simply not enough; there had to be, in addition, a reimagination of church for those with little or no connection to inherited patterns and rituals. That personal journey, over an hour and half, was clearly one of real pain. He saw the reality of the landscape. The valley. The bones. The dryness. He experienced it for himself and fell quiet at the truth of it. I felt a little guilty that I had been the cause of his grief. But of course, ultimately, I was glad. This process of honest truth-telling, which can be awkward, painful and uncomfortable, is hugely empowering. It is a lament that then begins to give way to new hope, a reimagined vision, a future doxology of God's goodness.

3

Entering a new story

He asked me 'Son of man, can these bones live?' I said, 'Sovereign Lord, you alone know.'
EZEKIEL 37:3

In Spain, in the middle of the 16th century, a young monk by the name of John joined the Convent of the Incarnation in Avila. This monastery had been started by Teresa of Avila at the beginning of a reformist movement within the Carmelite order. Building on reforms in other orders, Teresa had begun to establish new convents, and eventually monasteries, that advocated a return to the simple and contemplative life that had been the hallmark of the original Carmelite order. Teresa's reforms faced huge opposition, not only from nuns in the order, but also from the papal authorities. Consequently, John soon came under scrutiny for his involvement with the new movement.

In the winter of 1577, John was abducted from his home at the Incarnation, blindfolded and taken to a monastery in Toledo. He was jailed for nine months and subjected to severe physical deprivation and routine beatings. For much of this time, he was kept in solitary confinement in a cramped cell with only a slit in the door for any light or air. It was through this experience of darkness, complete isolation and uncertainty that John began to compose the poetic works that record and explore his spiritual journey, including his famous poem 'Dark Night of the Soul'.

Of the many insights of the theology of St John of the Cross' writings, perhaps the most fundamental is that it is only through the experience of darkness, in whatever guise that experience comes, that we are liberated from the things that hinder us from fully embracing the love of God. Dark night takes us to the end of our knowing, the end of our bravado, the end of our ego – it takes us to a place of uncertainty and questioning, of deep disorientation and confusion. Yet it also takes us to a place of surrender. And beyond surrender is the beginning of something new, for then, and often only then, can God meet us in a way that we will receive. In exile, Israel experienced a collective dark night. John's experience and resulting spiritual insights connect strongly with the history and literature that emerges from the exile.

One of the characteristics of the literature of the exile is the number of questions. Certainty and assertiveness seem to have given way to a different attitude which welcomes questions, often without directly answering them. The questions are real and relevant. They are signs of a dramatic shift in Israel's self-understanding. There is a vulnerability and a meekness signified by the intrusion of questions into the literature. All Israel's certainties and triumphs have been rendered valueless – there is little space for certainty now.

Another characteristic of the literature is the element of surprise. There is satire, mischief, subversion in this writing, where standard motifs are played with, reversed and adapted to make a point. It is as if they too are saying that Israel is in new territory here; the old ways of speaking about God, the old ways in which God might speak, are being questioned and challenged.

The book of Jonah, for example, begins in the classic formulaic manner of a book of prophecy: 'The word of the Lord came to Jonah...' (Jonah 1:1); except that the writer has inserted an extra word, lost to most English translations, a word which questions the standard motif completely: the little word 'now'. 'Now' is a word that belongs to different genre, the genre of storytelling. 'Now,' says the writer, as in 'once upon a time'; as in 'let me tell you a story about a prophet called Jonah'. So perhaps this isn't a book of prophecy at all, but a book *about* a prophet, a prophet who wrestles with his calling as God's instrument and representative, a prophet who descends into darkness and death and comes out the other side. And so begins a story that questions the standard assumptions about prophets, faith, obedience and vocation; not just of Jonah, but also of the people of God.

I wonder too whether the place of this question, 'Son of man, can these bones live?', within the book of Ezekiel is significant. The question is addressed to 'Son of man', which is the title by which Ezekiel is addressed throughout the book. The term simply means 'mortal'. It is not thought to connect with its use in Daniel or by Jesus. It is a term of address that leaves Ezekiel clear about his status in the relationship. And, throughout the book, 'Son of man' is followed almost invariably by an imperative, to do this or say that. 'Son of man' becomes a precursor to action of either practical demonstration or speech. It develops into a formulaic motif in the book for God's word through Ezekiel, using Ezekiel as a 'mortal man' and agency for his revelation to the exiles. There are a number of examples where the term is followed by a question,[32] though not with any answer from Ezekiel. These examples are more like rhetorical devices than genuine questions, questions that add to the justification God is giving for Ezekiel's subsequent instruction, rather than inviting genuine participation.

The question of chapter 37 is, however, a surprise. 'Son of man,' says the Spirit, 'can these bones live?' In one sense, this is surely also a rhetorical device. The answer, following Ezekiel's extensive tour, is obvious. Indeed, the Spirit's leading of Ezekiel to such an overwhelming confrontation with this vision of death was surely designed to make precisely this point. No, they can't live! There is no going back. The death of Israel's hopes and assumptions about life in God, the undeniability of this reality, is uncompromisingly conveyed by the horror tour of bones.

Commentators point out that the question also calls into play Ezekiel's faith in the supernatural power of God. Ezekiel's fundamental theology was of a God sovereign over life and death. Nothing in the realm of either earth or heaven was beyond his power or control. As Wright points out, Ezekiel would have known the stories from the ministries of Elijah and Elisha, stories of the resuscitation of the dead through prayer and through contact with the bones of Elisha.[33] Even so, this was an immense challenge to the faith of Ezekiel, fresh from the trauma of his experience of the dead army and armed with a few distant stories from his tradition.

But this casts the question too simply within a dualism of material and spiritual. In material terms, when asking for the reversal of utter death into new physical life, the answer is clearly 'no'. In spiritual terms, in view of God's sovereignty of all life in earth and heaven, the answer is 'yes'. But this is not a question designed to provide some binary choice between despair and triumph. The point of the question, as with other questions that populate the literature of exile, is not to elicit a right or wrong answer. This question is not a test, but an *invitation*. The question creates a space, in a way that none of the previous questions addressed to this 'Son of man' have done. There is genuine space here for Ezekiel to wrestle with the possibilities contained within it. And there is the real desire for Ezekiel to step into that space by venturing a response. This is not a technical question but a personal one. It is a question looking not for a rational answer, but a relational one. It is a question that seems to invite Ezekiel beyond knowing, deeper into the mystery of God's person. And it does that by offering Ezekiel a space, not between one knowing or another (material or spiritual), but *beyond* either.

So, while we might be led into thinking that this 'Son of man – question' motif was like the others before it, here the question is deliberate. It signals perhaps a new departure in the relationship between God and the prophet Ezekiel, a new invitation for Ezekiel to inhabit something beyond a kind of linear command and obedience and to enter into more of a dynamic relationship of participation with God.

Ezekiel's answer is a step into that mysterious space: 'Sovereign Lord, you alone know.' Contained in these few words is a significant statement of spiritual formation. It is an affirmation of God's sovereignty alongside the relinquishment of our own pretence at understanding or knowing. It has equivalents in other literature of exile. This is not unlike Jonah sitting in his booth at the edge of Nineveh, angry and confused at a God who does not act according to his assumptions, entering into a dialogue with God where it is God asking all the questions (Jonah 4). It is like Job, whose dogged insistence on taking his plea of innocence to God is met with a barrage of overwhelming and unanswerable question to which Job's response is one of exhausted submission: 'Surely I spoke of things I did not understand, things too wonderful for me to know' (Job 42:3b).

In each case, God has taken the person of faith to the very edge of their structured knowledge, to the place where light and certainty give way to darkness and unknowing. In these liminal places, the invitation is always to keep going, to relinquish the assurance of whatever ground beneath our feet we have relied on in terms of our theology, our practice, our status and our identity, and venture onwards with only God as our support and guide. We will rarely if ever go to such places ourselves, even if we are at all suspicious that we may need to. Instead, we must be led. That leading may well be painful, confusing, traumatic; it will confront us with harsh realities; it will illuminate the subconscious world of denial we have been playing in. And then the Spirit will ask us a question – 'Can these bones live?' This question exposes our feeble hopes and invites us into a richer paradigm of life that is beyond our knowing.

Exile and the way of the dark night

I have also experienced something of what it is to be led to the precipice between one paradigm and another. Leading a missional community, beyond the safety and security of the established structure of the church, took me to that place. I found that I had exhausted my own assumptions, models and techniques and felt I was getting nowhere. It was only then that I sensed my personal liminal question inviting me deeper into a leadership that welcomed uncertainty and unknowing. The question for me was a simple, 'Do you trust me?' And I realised I didn't, not really. I trusted the theology, the ecclesiology and the latest missional methods that I had read about. I trusted my intellect and my leadership abilities, and my ability to build a team and focus its energies in a fruitful direction. But I didn't trust God, not really.

It was the vulnerability involved in working without structure and in the context of a host environment (not always a welcoming one) that brought the question to the foreground. In going beyond the structures and resources of inherited church, I ventured into territory where I was dependent on the hospitality and generosity of others. The established ministry paradigm of the church has been one of enterprise – we work up our vision, gather our resources, formulate our strategy and set off. It is a paradigm developed in an established context where we can rely on safety, plenty and power. My ministry took me into a place of vulnerability and scarcity. We had no building, few people and no plan for what would emerge from our presence in the wider community. In that context, we learned to trust and I gradually learned to lead in a posture of surrender and vulnerability that allowed the purposes of God to emerge.

Through this journey, I have found the concept of the 'dark night' extremely fruitful. The essence of the 'dark night' is not so much an experience of pain, but one of uncertainty. The word translated 'dark' is the Spanish word *oscura* which literally means 'obscure'. At its heart, the experience of 'dark night' is an experience of obscurity, of unknowing, in which the familiar resources with which we navigate our life, inner as well as outer, are lost to us.

The great insight and treasure of John of the Cross' experience and subsequent writing is that this experience is a gift: a gift from God. Dark night is that space in which God leads us gently to a place of surrender and relinquishment, where the things that give us security and safety are sifted and scrutinised.[34] They are subjected to the test of idolatry; our grip on them, conscious or unconscious, is loosened. In this place we are set free, free from those attachments and distractions that have been false idols and empty assurances for us. We are freed towards a renewed and deeper relationship with God. John's great insight about the experience of dark night might be summarised like this:

> It is the secret way in which God not only liberates us from our attachments and idolatries, but also brings us to the realisation of our true nature. The night is the means by which we find our heart's desire, our freedom for love.[35]

For Israel, all that had constituted their known world has been lost – not only lost but discredited and mocked. All the furniture of Israel's communal life, the 'symbols and props which held life together'[36] had been destroyed. This moment in history became a key point of transition, with the key prophets of the time (Ezekiel, Jeremiah and second Isaiah) articulating a renewal not based, as before, on continued appeals to the assumptions of the past, but instead on welcoming a new work of God. Brueggemann summarises this disjunction of the story of Israel as a point of 'relinquishment and receiving'.[37] The exile is the point of death and resurrection in the Old Testament. It is the moment the very fabric of Israel's life and faith, its body of tradition and custom, is taken to the grave in order that there might be a resurrection into a new way of being.

Furthermore, it becomes clear that, in much the same way as John saw 'dark night' as part of the grace of God, exile also came to be seen as God's action in the life of Israel. These same prophets make it clear that, as much as the exile is the result of growing Babylonian power, it is also the action of God. Exile is the path that Israel takes into the dark night, the path that invites them to relinquish their hold on idols and attachments and find freedom for that new thing God is doing among them.

The dark night of the church

Some have suggested that, in much the same way, the church in the west is also going through its own dark night. Our own story of exile has led to similar experiences and responses as those of Israel. Our denial can sound like those voices advocating a return to old certainties and patterns of life: the faithful exposition of the word, the confident celebration of the Eucharist, the commitment to the parish system, the holding on to traditional buildings. We might also see the threat of assimilation in the church's commitment to the ambiguous value of relevance. Here, it might be easy to critique the church's endless debates over human sexuality which run along the fault lines of pastoral compassion, missional credibility and biblical faithfulness. However, the greatest threat in terms of assimilation is predominantly in the attitude of our communities to money, time and possessions. If worshipping Yahweh in Babylon was a direct challenge to Marduk, the worship of Jesus Christ is primarily a challenge to the idols of consumerism and materialism, which put a price on everything, recruit everything into a religion of 'more' and leave adherents endlessly unsatisfied, unremittingly busy and constantly exhausted.

In this experience of exile, the church faces a challenge that is far more radical than that which can be solved by a few tweaks here and there. As one writer puts it:

> There are times when whole communities of people lose sight of the sun in ways that unnerve them. This seems to be happening to a lot of church people right now… While they experiment with new worship styles and set up Facebook pages, most of them know that the problem runs deeper than that. The old ways of being Christian are not working anymore… Something in the old ways has died, or is dying – truly a great cause for sorrow, even among those who know the time has come – and yet at the same time something is being born.[38]

Changes in liturgy or worship style might suggest a quick fix and might be within the reach of our capabilities and resources, but they will not be enough. Similarly, organisational changes, the default response to many a time of crisis, will not work – 'You cannot restructure your way out of Babylon.'[39]

Exile as an experience of 'dark night' invites the church instead to a posture of 'relinquishment and receiving', which is inspired primarily by the question, 'Can these bones live?' – an invitation to venture into a new kind of participative space in which there is a surrendered openhandedness to that new thing God might be doing.

Leading in the land beyond

It might be tempting in the light of this to apply this attitude of relinquishment to our own diagnoses of the church's predicament – particular liturgies, costly buildings, professional clergy, specific doctrines of the atonement, entrenched attitudes towards women and certain sexual ethics are often seen as necessarily dispensable. But in terms of our study of exile and of Ezekiel, one of the key transitions is in the arena of leadership. This moment and statement of surrender is a moment of relinquishment and the beginning of receiving a new kind of leadership for Ezekiel and for Israel.

Ezekiel's journey from a young ordinand in Jerusalem to this moment is a personal leadership journey through the dark night of Israel's exile. It is a journey from assumptions about status and authority as a priest in the religious tradition of Israel, through the loss of that whole world and his calling as a prophet, to this moment where a new landscape opens up. The invitation of God at that moment is one beyond the settled structures and patterns of either priest or prophet, towards something less linear, predictable and formulaic, and towards a more creative, surprising and participatory kind of leadership with God's Spirit in the renewal of his people.

Posture here is a key word, for in our quest for answers and solutions, we forget that what is really required is a change in our fundamental spirituality of ministry as a people. This in turn is expressed in terms of our attitude and our stance in the dynamic relationship between ourselves, God and the world around us. The key characteristics of posture arrived are, in the words of Ezekiel, 'Sovereign Lord, only you know' – that is, humility, restraint and attentiveness. These characteristics shape a leadership beyond the dominant paradigms of the status quo.

'**Sovereign Lord...**' Humility is a function of the right view of our status through an appropriate view of the status of others. The phrase 'Sovereign Lord' is used throughout Ezekiel. It is now being used as it was always meant to be used: as a term of worship. There is great danger in leadership of using terms of God's power and authority for our own uses, of using such phrases or their equivalents as a means to impress God upon our authority, or lack of it. It is the testimony of Ezekiel that God is free to be who he will be; he will not be used. Western culture has arrived at a place where everything must have its use. This is a culture of doing, not being. Those things that assert a nature of pure being are invariably pressed into co-option in some utilitarian purpose. God likewise has been co-opted into our political or missional plans, shoring up our uncertainties in the midst of the dark night of our culture and our church. Ministry, too, is essentially utilitarian, with the pressure to perform, to generate results and outcomes and to assert our usefulness through the language of busy-ness.

> All of us are too busy being useful. The more there is to worry about professional and institutional survival, the more useful we seek to be. Indeed our usefulness is only related remotely to the reality of ministry. Such an effort at usefulness may rob us of vitality.[40]

The relinquishment of our own pretences, power and plans brings us to a place of humility. It is a place where we begin to 'accept God's being as God's will'.[41] That is, moving beyond a utilitarian image of God who might add something of a blessing to our concepts and plans, to an embracing of the mysterious participatory and missionary nature of the Trinity within which we are invited to live. In this place, a 'willed passivity'[42] can bring about a more integrated participation with the person of God in the will of God. This place is the landscape beyond enterprise, beyond fantasy, beyond working harder at the same things in the hope of achieving better results.

'... only you know.' Restraint is related to humility in that it is about knowing the limitations of our leadership and ministry. One of the great pressures of leadership in our knowledge-obsessed culture is to be concerned with what people ask or expect you to know. Our own reformist traditions in this country grew out of a noble movement towards the democratisation of knowledge through the translation and distribution of the scriptures. The western Christian tradition, influenced hugely by the Enlightenment, has been informed by the pursuit of knowledge. Meanwhile, the acceptance of not knowing – or what is called the apophatic tradition – is more associated with the eastern and Russian Orthodox churches. The way the western church prepares its leaders has settled on essentially an academic path which is oriented more towards the accumulation of knowledge and its application. Yet the very basis of calling and vocation is to yield ourselves into a place of not knowing, into a journey through unknown territory, where our knowledge will not be predicated on the ability to rehearse or apply knowledge from some hidden store, but through God's revelation – 'Go... to the land *I will show you*' (Genesis 12:1, italics mine).

Accepting a more apophatic way, a way of embracing the limitations of knowledge, evokes a leadership that enhances people's sense of responsibility. It guards us against and saves us from our attachment to control. 'For us and for our salvation there are times when life must enter a cloud of unknowing where words and thoughts have no means of taking control.'[43]

If I could describe our missional community to you, it would be a group of Christians trying to work out how to take appropriate responsibility *together* for their discipleship and mission. In the early church and the emergent missional churches throughout history, a key factor in their vitality and growth is the responsibility of the whole community in ministry, and the lack of educated leadership. The curve of Methodist membership in America was exponential to the point when one in three Americans were Methodist, and then it trailed away steadily to the present day. The inflection on this curve coincides with the point in Methodist history when they started formally educating people for Methodist leadership.[44] Without a leader, educated and placed in a community to lead in ways that others are assumed not to be able to, these communities are environments in which the ministerial responsibility of the whole community and a thirst for God's leading and direction become normative.

Ezekiel's acceptance of 'not knowing' is a result of his lament and surrender in the valley of the bones, but it is also a leadership posture that has grown through his journey from establishment priest to dissident prophet. Ezekiel's ministry demonstrates a 'decentred' leadership that recognises the limitations of his ministry. It is a restraint based on the acceptance and observance of God's holiness, the glory of who he is. 'He is clear in the midst of his relentlessness about what he is charged to do and not to do. He must not do less, but also he need not do more. He must let God have his relentless way.'[45]

If, in our own leadership, we are to emulate this posture of restraint, we must similarly surrender the expectations and responsibilities that are placed on us by our training and, so often, by the collusion we fall into between ourselves and those we lead. Leadership must be a constant discipline in keeping open the space in which God may speak and others may take responsibility. It is therefore the constant discipline of restraint, of being clear what is ours to do and the discipline of not doing what others might do in the pursuit of their own growth and flourishing.

'**... you know**'. This relates closely to the final characteristic, which is that of attentiveness. Surrendering our own addiction to rational knowledge, and opening up to the desperate need to base our lives and ministry on the knowledge of God, lead us to seeking that knowledge above all else. But of course, this knowledge is of a different nature altogether; this is knowledge through an attention to God's person, God's presence, not so much God's opinion or plan. Wanting to know God just so we might know his will is surely just another way of making God a utility. What Ezekiel instead presents is a knowledge of God sought through attention to the holiness of God. The whole book reflects on the traumatic moment of the loss of God's presence from the temple and the return of his glory towards the end. While Israel is distracted by false prophecies, pointless allegiances and other gods in a bid for survival, the presence of God leaves the temple and leaves Jerusalem to the fate the people of God have chosen for it. The hope of the return of God's presence is not so much connected with a restoration of all that has been lost, but on God's fidelity and holiness. It is because of who he is that there is hope, not because of anything God may or may not do. So 'Ezekiel is not preoccupied with hope but with holiness. Perhaps hope will follow when holiness is rightly discerned.'[46]

Attentiveness and leading through attentiveness are closely related, then, to silence. It always seems that leadership in today's church brings the expectation of having rather a lot to say, when, in fact, we might do well to reflect on whether the call to lead is the call to silence, out of which a more restrained and humble speech might emerge. Ezekiel's answer is essentially a leaning towards silence. He does not have an answer; he does not have anything to say. His response is to acknowledge that the only speech worth attending to at this point is that of God. In our leadership, we can attend to God in silence in a number of ways. There is the foundational discipline of silent prayer, which increasingly for me is the commitment to begin each day simply attending to God's presence in silence; I often do this at other points in the day too. This discipline curbs my drift towards mindless speech and trains my soul to depend on the presence of God.

Attentiveness and silence also extend outward in our commitment to listening to God's voice among those we lead, and beyond there to the communities and context in which we minister. If exile teaches us anything, it is that the presence of God is not confined to the supposed limits of our rituals and our imaginations. That Ezekiel's theophany took place in a desolate valley remote from the exilic communities of Babylon, far from a destroyed and redundant temple in Jerusalem, shows what he and this community were learning about their assumption about how, when and where God could be present and God could speak.

Finally, attentiveness and silence are not somehow an earning of the right to speak. This posture of leadership does not invite the re-emergence of the leader in the manner of Moses returning from the mountain, ready to dispense edicts and commandments. The role of our attentiveness is to foster attentiveness in others. Twice in the book of Ezekiel, God charges him as a 'watchman' for the house of Israel (3:16–19 and 33:7–9). The role assigned to him is to watch and to warn: to hear God's voice, to speak it and then to leave the people to respond in their own capacity. In other words, the role of watchman is to point people to the source of that which you have been called to be attentive to. The leader cannot have faith *for* people, cannot be responsible for what people do in their own response to the presence of God; a leader can only watch, listen and point those they lead to the same presence, the same voice that is the basis of their own life and leadership.

One short verse lies between the valley of death and desolation, and the beginnings of a vision of hope. It is a verse that acts as a hinge within a hinge. The book of Ezekiel can be split essentially into two parts (chapters 1—14 and 33—48), with an interlude between them containing various prophecies directed towards other nations. The first section is essentially a reflection on the reasons for exile, a critique of the idolatrous practices of Jerusalem, which constructs a powerful argument for Israel's culpability in the destruction of the city. The pivot around which the book turns comes in chapter 33: 'A man who had escaped from Jerusalem came to me and said, "The city has fallen!"' (v. 21).

Thereafter, the focus is beyond the fall of the city and towards the emergence of hope. The valley of dry bones repeats this pattern; it is a retrospective of the fall of Jerusalem, which lays out in lurid detail the horror and finality, but which also contains within it details that point to judgement, opens a way towards the new and the hopeful. But only when this confrontation and critique has brought Ezekiel to a place of surrender and silence does the landscape open up in which God can do a new thing. There must be death before there can be any resurrection; there must be a death of the hope of resuscitation or restoration before the hope of resurrection can be embraced.

4

Living to a different script

Then he said to me, 'Prophesy to these bones and say to them, "Dry bones, hear the word of the Lord! This is what the Sovereign Lord says to these bones: I will make breath enter you, and you will come to life. I will attach tendons to you and make flesh come upon you and cover you with skin; I will put breath in you, and you will come to life. Then you will know that I am the Lord."'

So I prophesied as I was commanded. And as I was prophesying, there was a noise, a rattling sound, and the bones came together, bone to bone. I looked, and tendons and flesh appeared on them and skin covered them, but there was no breath in them.

Then he said to me, 'Prophesy to the breath; prophesy, son of man, and say to it, "This is what the Sovereign Lord says: come, breath, from the four winds and breathe into these slain, that they may live."' So I prophesied as he commanded me, and breath entered them; they came to life and stood up on their feet – a vast army.

Then he said to me: 'Son of man, these bones are the people of Israel. They say, "Our bones are dried up and our hope is gone; we are cut off." Therefore, prophesy and say to them: "This is what the Sovereign Lord says: My people, I am going to open your graves and bring you up from them; I will bring you back to the land of Israel. Then you, my people, will know that I am the Lord, when I open your graves and bring you up from them. I will put my Spirit in you and you will live, and I will settle you in your own land. Then you will know that I the Lord have spoken, and I have done it, declares the Lord."'

EZEKIEL 37:4–14

Pioneer ministry is still a relatively new ordained vocation in the Church of England. It has struggled to be understood and being, in its nature, a ministry at the edges of the institution, has not always found it easy to make its voice heard. More recently, a working definition of pioneer ministry has been produced by the central church, which has provided the basis for a helpful conversation on the nature of this ministry:

Pioneers are people called by God who are the first to see and creatively respond to the Holy Spirit's initiatives with those outside the church; gathering those around them as they seek to establish new contextual Christian community.[47]

The call of God into the new is a dynamic relationship between awareness and the Holy Spirit. Pioneering is not primarily some kind of new technique. It may well be possible to describe it in these terms, to break it down into a set of practices, even to write a manual for the uninitiated.[48] But fundamentally, standing like Ezekiel in liminal places and looking to enable the new thing that is so desperately needed is not essentially a matter of doing, but a matter of seeing. And seeing is a business of the soul, the spirit, a fruit of the long journey of faithful commitment to God.

Pioneers are 'the first to see'. But what kind of seeing is that? Pioneers are not the only ones with the ability to see. There are plenty of people who can 'see what needs doing here'. When I first started as a pioneer minister ten years ago, I arrived naively enthusiastic and slightly clueless in a town that was unknown to me, and in which I had been somewhat heralded as representing a hope for the future. I had no shortage of people who had been 'first to see' and who were quite happy to pass on their visions to me for their execution. On the whole, these visions, which I did my best to listen graciously to, were of the 'enterprising project' variety. They were a fusion of anxiety, need and the internet. Most involved a success story plucked from another church somewhere else inserted into the missional activity of our local community.

Instead, the sort of seeing referred to in this definition is the one implied by the second idea: 'and creatively respond to the Holy Spirit's initiative'. The kind of seeing that renewal invites is not a purely logical or strategic 'gap in the market'. It is not a franchise opportunity. It is the kind of seeing that only occurs when we let go of our pet images and ego-inspired projections and look to respond to the envisioning of the Holy Spirit.

The Holy Spirit's envisioning in the valley of dry bones is the unfolding of a vision of hope for Israel. Initially, one could be forgiven for seeing the beginnings of this vision as restoration, that is, a reversal, a return to the visions of hope from before the exile. Surely the whole point of the tour of the bones was to discredit this false hope? And yet God's words to Ezekiel, to which he responds obediently, appear to remember (literally 're-member') this army and the hope that it represents. Bones miraculously reform and come together. Skin and flesh form on them. There is a reversal of the life–death pattern. The army looks set to return.

Yet one essential thing is missing from them: 'There was no breath in them' (v. 8). The second stage of the unfolding vision therefore involves Ezekiel invoking breath from the 'four winds' to 'breathe into these slain, that they may live' (v. 9). And, like someone revived from drowning, or like a newborn sucking in its first breath, the reassembled bodies were animated by this breath. They 'stood up on their feet – a vast army' (v. 10). Again, on first reading it appears that we have simply reversed the narrative. We are back to where we appear to have started: with a vast army ready to be deployed to save Israel from its domination by foreign powers. However, the two-stage development of the vision and the singular role of 'breath' suggests something very different, something more like recreation, even resurrection.

The creation narrative of Genesis 2, for example, takes shape in a similar way. Firstly, 'the Lord God formed a man from the dust of the ground' (2:7a). But, while the form of the human is apparently complete, a second stage is needed: God 'breathed into his nostrils the breath of life' and only then can man be declared 'a living being' (2:7b). Here in the valley of Ezekiel 37, as in the garden of Genesis 2, lifeless dust is formed by God into a human form and then the vital ingredient of divine breath completes the process of creation. This suggests, then, in the case of the vast army, not so much resuscitation but recreation. And, as in Genesis 2, the momentum of creation is not backwards but forwards. Genesis begins with a declaration of the beginning of time, making clear that all that takes place after that is the onward unfolding of the action of God *in time*. The days are marked off with the momentum of counting – 'And there was evening, and there was morning – the first day' (literally 'day one', Genesis 1:5). The poetry is structured to express the creation of a circling rhythm of days including the sabbath, but also to express the agency of God, which is always forward and always creative.

The creation taking place in Ezekiel 37, of course, offers a foretaste of the new creation and throws us, as well as backwards, *forward to the resurrection*. Once again, we are in a place of bones, of the dead, at the edge of a city governed by foreign and pagan forces, and in which the people of Israel are displaced and struggling to assert their identity and autonomy. John makes clear his allusions to the creation story. We are in a garden (19:41) on the first day of the week (20:1). Jesus emerges from the tomb in the form of a human being and yet displays characteristics that are beyond human, walking through material walls, appearing and disappearing frequently and across great distances. And breath is once again a feature of the narrative. After the appearance to Mary Magdalene in the garden, John's narrative takes us to the disciples, exiled by their own fear to a single room. Into their exile, Jesus appeared, 'breathed on them and said, "Receive the Holy Spirit"' (John 20:22). These are striking parallels, and Wright therefore sees in Ezekiel at this moment the foreshadowing of the person of Christ in the dawning of a new age:

> The most significant echo of Ezekiel 37 comes in a locked room on the very evening of his resurrection, when, we read, 'He breathed on them and said, "Receive the Holy Spirit."' The Lord of life himself, freshly risen to his feet from where he had lain among the bones of the dead, adopts simultaneously the posture of Ezekiel in summoning the breath of God, and the posture of God himself in commanding the breath of the Spirit to come upon the disciples.[49]

John's recounting of the resurrection story is expressed in terms of creation, recreation. But clearly recreation does not mean the reversing of creation, a winding back of the clock to some preternatural bliss. The recreation that is resurrection throws us forward to the new age, the new heaven and the new earth that are being created from the material of the old.

That this is a resurrection event is made even more clear when the scene shifts to the graveyard (Ezekiel 37:11–14): 'I am going to open your graves and bring you up from them,' says the Lord. The verb translated 'bring you up' is the same as that used elsewhere to refer to the exodus (e.g. 1 Samuel 12:6; Hosea 12:13). In other words, this 'bringing up' from the grave is more than resuscitation – it is the renewal of life followed by the creation of a new kind of life, free from the slavery and oppression of the past.[50]

The life of this new creation is made possible by 'breath', identified clearly as the Holy Spirit. Where the Spirit is, there is life and freedom. And where the Spirit is, there is the newness of God's creative intent, a newness beyond our stale categories and our nostalgic preference for imagining hope in inherited terms, a newness that invites, a newness that surprises and disarms.

So Ezekiel's invitation is to participate in resurrection, not renovation. The material of this new creation will be that of the old, but the key agency of 'breath' means that we should expect something surprisingly different to that which our traditional paradigms might suggest.

Come, four winds...

'Breath' is just one translation of the Hebrew word *ruach*. In fact, *ruach* infuses the entire passage. The word is used no less than ten times. It is the Spirit of the Lord (37:1) that brings Ezekiel into the valley in the beginning that will live in the people of Israel in the fulfilment of the vision. *Ruach* is translated 'breath' four times in the central prophecy of the passage. But it also has the sense of 'wind', as in the atmospheric movement of air, and this sense is used in the summoning of the 'four winds' (v. 9). It is in this central verse that three senses, slightly overlapping, are used virtually simultaneously: 'This is what the Sovereign Lord says: Come, breath, from the four winds and breathe into these slain, that they may live' (v. 9). A physical gathering of winds from the four corners of the earth, appears to constitute the presence of the divine Spirit which is able in itself to generate life where there has been death.

The multivalency and ambiguity of the language itself has the effect of conveying the nature of the renewal process that Ezekiel is participating in. Beyond the political and military forms of renewal that Israel might imagine is the possibility of renewal based on the holiness of God and his Holy Spirit. What the language will not allow us to do, however, is make this a tidy process. It will resist all efforts at systematising – though we will no doubt have a jolly good try! It is the testimony of so many movements of the Spirit that they have too often been domesticated and formularised in the vain hope of controlling what is too wild for our liking. Perhaps it can be no other way. Organisational form is necessary; it is hard to live otherwise. But if this vision of renewal in the context of exile suggests anything, it is that when all institutional life has been wiped off the map, we are being invited to live in relation to an uncomfortably form-averse God in order to see life emerge from death.

Perhaps, too, the story is about relinquishing our seduction with the organisations and institutions that are the apparent providers of life and success in the world. Israel's exile might well be traced back to that moment when it asked for 'a king to lead us, such as all the other nations have' (1 Samuel 8:5). Samuel, in reply, warned them of the consequences of their request. All that this institution promised was not necessarily good. There were costs and pitfalls that needed to be heeded. But the seduction of a form that promised power and peace was too great to resist. Israel's exile is the child of that affair with institutional power, come home to roost. The resurrection of the slain army acknowledges, perhaps, the need for organisation, for structure and for form. But insistent and thorough animation with the breath of the Spirit advocates for a willingness to receive unpredictability, adaptability, movement rather than monument, organism rather than organisation. As John V. Taylor succinctly puts it: 'The Holy Spirit does not appear to have read the rubric'.[51]

In post-Christendom, where the church as a locus of institutional influence and power has been marginalised and discredited, we are nevertheless seduced in our anxiety and laziness to import the strategies and techniques of our culture in the hope of renewal. Capitalism has succeeded in commodifying everything, including experience. A culture that has most things it needs, as well as a huge number of things it doesn't, must be enticed to continue consuming something. So, rather than the material, it must be marketed as the ephemeral. These experiences are packaged as pivotal moments of salvation and hope in a starved and dreary world.

I wonder, though, whether the rush towards resource-hungry churches that major on structures of event experiences and programmes plays into this temptation. The young-adult culture that we are rapidly losing touch with might well be drawn to the fleeting offers of the consumer market, but we have lost our nerve if all we can do is try and compete on the same terms. Research suggests that this same generation yearns for the solid, the authentic, the lasting. It yearns for community and purpose.[52] We are offering 'bread and circuses', much like the wider culture, when quietly this generation has sussed the inconsistencies and shallowness of much of the world and longs for something of substance.

Likewise, the domination of business in our world, exemplified by the protrusion of gleaming glass-clad corporate towers in every major city, far exceeding the spires and towers of Christendom, casts a powerful spell. We have eaten off the table of corporate culture for some time now, importing its strategies, five-year plans, targets and outcomes, casting Jesus as CEO, sending our church leaders on MBAs and treating our congregations like shareholder investors who must be kept happy and docile by our consistent performance and excellence in the spotlight. It is not that we are ignorant of our theology and have consciously swapped service, participation and real-life, whole-life discipleship for a corporate experience. Rather, we have found ourselves colluding with one another and with a culture that too often integrates neat systems and ordered programmes over the discomforting and unsettling presence of the Holy Spirit. Renewal must involve relinquishment. It must involve loss. For many churches, there is a great deal to lose before a Spirit of wildness and unpredictability can truly be embraced.

The key thing is that looking towards the false gods of our culture distracts us from the primary awareness we need: an awareness of the Holy Spirit. We are so busy with the operational demands of offering experiences, running programmes or executing strategic plans that we simply do not enter into the kind of undistracted space in which we can truly be attentive to God's Spirit. Yet that is what this vision of Ezekiel is about: it is an invitation from God to inhabit a new kind of participative space where God's Spirit is at the front and centre of life.

An invitation to the drama

The whole prophecy of Ezekiel 37:4–14 has a repetitive, insistent quality about it, with repeated motifs and phrases providing structure and form to the passage. The arrangement of these motifs and elements is in a form that offers an insight into its interpretation:

'Then he said to me, "Prophesy… and say"' (v. 4)
   Oracle of hope ('I will' x 3) (vv. 5–6)
     'Then you will know that I am the Lord' (v. 6b)
   'So I prophesied as I was commanded' (v. 7)
Oracle of hope fulfilled (vv. 7b–8)

'Then he said to me, "Prophesy… and say"' (v. 9)
   Oracle of instruction (v. 9b)
     'That they may live' (v. 9c)
   'So I prophesied as he commanded me' (v. 10a)
Oracle of instruction fulfilled (v. 10b)

'A vast army' = the people of Israel whose hope is gone (v. 10c–11)

'Therefore prophesy and say' (v. 12a)
   Oracle of hope ('I will' x 4) (vv. 12b–14)
     'Then you will know that I the Lord have spoken' (v. 14b)

Arranging the material in this way provides an insight into the flow and intent of the vision. Firstly, it emphasises **the priority of God's initiative**. The material arranges into three distinct sections each propelled by the initiating word of God. Once again, there are echoes here of creation, with the momentum of renewal moved forward by the repeated motif: 'Then he said' (compare 'And God said' in Genesis 1). Then in the first and third sections, the primacy of God's action is emphasised by the repeated refrain 'I will/I am going to'. Seven times in all this simple phrase is repeated: three in the first section and a further four in the third. I have called these sections oracles of hope. Israel has strived for so long to save itself through means of the popular salvation narratives of the day. To find true hope, it must finally yield to the 'I will' of God.

Secondly, in both of these sections containing an oracle of hope, the result is clear: 'Then you will know that I am the Lord.' What is made eminently clear is that the aim of the vision is to reassert **the priority of God's identity**. There might be two readings of the phrase depending on where the emphasis lands. Both are apt. 'Then you will know that *I* am the Lord' suggests that the result must be a rejection of all other pretenders to lordship and sovereignty, a relinquishment of all the feeble gods that have wheedled their way into Israel's pantheon, and a re-enthronement of God as Lord. But in addition, 'Then you will know that I am the *Lord*' has equal power. Israel has been guilty of domesticating God to their own demands and anxieties. Renewal and hope can only come through a relinquishment of this tendency to make God a servant to our agendas and schemes. God must be free to be God. He is not God *for* anything. He is God whose person and lordship is enough for us to trust and depend on for all our hopes. In his assessment of Ezekiel as a voice to the exiles, Brueggemann focuses on the phrase 'For the sake of my holy name' as indicative of what the whole book is about. Ezekiel's message is essentially that hope must be founded on the very nature of God, on his 'name', not on his ability to do for us what we would dearly love him to do: 'All hope for the future rests in the very character of God, for this God will take seriously being God.'[53]

Thirdly, the material makes clear the **invitation to participation**. This participation is always in response to God's initiative. Our posture in the flow of God's renewal is not one of passivity, as though whatever we do is nothing in the light of God's action, nor over-activity, as though all depends on us and without us little would happen. Instead, our posture is like that of someone always on the threshold of instruction and action.

Some years ago, I spent a year in Africa living in a remote part of Kenya, where our local journeys were dependent on buses that ran to little or no discernible timetable. Waiting for a bus was a constant part of our lives. When I returned home and lived for a while in London, it was around the time when bus stops introduced digital displays to tell you how long you would be left waiting until your next bus arrived. I noticed how differently I waited in London compared with the hours of waiting in Kenya. In London, I waited without urgency or attentiveness for something that, when it came, was wholly unsurprising. In Kenya, I waited with my senses trained to the bend in the road or the brow of the hill from where the bus would at some point emerge. It was a constantly attentive practice of waiting, leaning in to the ever-present possibility that this would be the moment when action would be required.

This is the attitude of our participation in the renewing work of God and the form of these passages invites us to welcome this posture as a path to the fulfilment of the vision. In both the first two sections, Ezekiel tells us 'I prophesied as I was commanded' and what has been prophesied comes to pass. But now, in the last section, there is departure from the repeated structure of the unfolding vision. Two things happen to make a break with the first section.

Firstly, the scene of the vision moves from the battlefield to the graveyard. The vast army has been renewed (v. 10) but, as the scene changes, the Spirit widens the vision to equate this army with the whole of Israel. The failure of Israel cannot be blamed on a lack of military might. It is not just a result of shifting geopolitical circumstances. 'These bones are *the people of Israel.*' Everyone is responsible. Consequently, the widening vision, with an even clearer imagery of resurrection as the dead house of Israel is lifted from the grave, will involve the whole community.

The second break with the structure is in the lack of fulfilment. The final section ends without resolution. It ends with a final statement of the repeated refrain, 'Then you will know that I the Lord have spoken', which in previous sections has resulted in obedience to the instruction to prophesy, followed by fulfilment. However, here the statement is made without response. The vision comes to an open end, like a poem missing its final rhyming couplet or music ending on an imperfect cadence. The vision ends like an unfinished symphony awaiting someone to step into the space and the silence. What is the implication of this? Surely it is that a response is waiting to be made. Ezekiel has demonstrated what is required: an alert attentiveness to the Spirit which results in action. The invitation is for an equivalent response from the house of Israel. There can be no reliance any more on institutions: the army, the monarchy, the priesthood, the prophets. The invitation now is to all Israel to indwell the Spirit (v. 14) and live in this dynamic, participative relationship with God through his Holy Spirit.

A participative church

God's initiative and identity are primal. Everyone is responsible. Everyone gets to take part. These are the key messages arising from this vision. Israel has domesticated God but, 'for the sake of my holy name' and so that 'then you will know that I am the Lord', God will enable the democratisation of his presence, inviting all of Israel to be carriers of the presence of God and participators in the renewing work of God. It is much as it was on the day of Pentecost: a system that organised access to God's forgiveness and presence, through complex systems of regulation and segregation, had been disrupted by the ministry, death and resurrection of Jesus whose promise to 'destroy the temple' (that symbol of the hope of restoration in a continued experience of exile) and 'raise it again in three days' had been fulfilled – only not at all in the way anyone expected. What came next was that same giving of the Spirit to include everyone in the purposes of God. So Peter can declare that was happening was a fulfilment of the God's vision through Joel whereby:

'I will pour out my Spirit on *all people*.
Your *sons and daughters* will prophesy,
your *young men* will see visions,

> your *old men* will dream dreams.
> Even on my *servants, both men and women*,
>   I will pour out my Spirit in those days.'
> ACTS 2:17–18 (italics mine)

Yet in our own day, we are just as guilty of resisting this invitation to participation and the leading of the Spirit in favour of our own various forms of organisation and legislation. And, indeed, the whole of church history might be viewed as a repeating cycle of Israel's predicament – how to journey with the untamed nature of the presence of God without domesticating him for our own uses.

This therefore begs the question of whether there is any structure (it's hard to live without it) that facilitates the sort of participative life of the Spirit and guards against the tendency towards domestication and control. John V. Taylor explores this same question in his wonderful book, *The Go-Between God* (SCM, 1972). His starting point in answering the question is a reflection on the nature of the early church as a fruit of the work of the Spirit. The spiritual renewal produced by the Holy Spirit in the early church is demonstrated by the emergence of the wild, communal and egalitarian nature of the early church. The New Testament is by no means a hagiography to the early church. The same controlling tendencies soon emerge: the debate around circumcision at the Jerusalem Council and the emergence of hierarchy in the Corinthian church, to name just a couple. But within the chaos, a consistent testimony of Holy Spirit community can be discerned which for Taylor can be seen in the Greek word *allelon*, 'one another'. 'One another' is scattered throughout the New Testament 'like a peal of bells'.[54] 'One another' is, if you like, proof that the Spirit's democratising power and work is at large, structuring (if that is the right word) the people of God as a bottom-up organic community in which the Spirit dwells.

In which case, says Taylor, 'the ideal shape of the church is such as will provide this "one-another-ness" with the least possible withdrawal of Christians from their corporateness with their fellow men in the world'.[55] That shape and size will likely be small. The testimony of the New Testament is for the existence of these small communities in response to the work of the Holy Spirit and the missionary context and nature of the church. They are therefore an argument for the life of these small communities now. Taylor calls these small communities the 'little congregations' and argues that their being small is precisely so that they are able to better respond to what the Spirit is doing in the world.

The church has been experimenting with these small communities, these 'little congregations', for a very long time, from the Celtic missionary bands, the early Franciscans, to the Lollards, the Wesleyan classes, the house church movement, cell church and now missional communities. And while this lengthy history suggests that the dialogue (if not a wrestling) between the 'little congregations' and the organisation of the church into normative and powerful forms is 'just the way it is', I want to argue for the essential renewing force that small communities of Spirit-attentive disciples are.

For it is in their smallness that the 'little congregations' protect the value of participation, remaining at a size when we can be in meaningful relationship with one another as a Christian community. This guards the kind of space which enables us to be attentive to the Spirit at work in our midst. The dynamic between people and the Holy Spirit when we can genuinely be 'one another' in community is one that gives space for the dynamic, dancing Spirit of God to move and be witnessed among us. It means that attentiveness is not the preserve of those in the know, or those whose role it is to know everyone, to have a leader's-eye-view of things. Instead, attentiveness is fostered throughout by mutual and equal relationship and the mutual indwelling of the Spirit. Christian community becomes a participative school for growing in attentiveness to the Holy Spirit.

Furthermore, when a 'little congregation' or missional community lives out their life in the midst of the world, in a particular neighbourhood or network, its size guards against the way in which the church so easily delegates the call to listen to the Spirit at work in the world to a caste of experts or professionals. The mutuality of participation, the one-another-ness of Christian community, extends into the community in which it is placed and with which it lives in dynamic missional dialogue. It is through the intimacy of community and storytelling day by day, week by week, that a community can be constantly attentive to the Spirit and adapt its life to it. 'It is the "little congregations" which must become normative *if the church is to respond to the Spirit's movement in the life of the world.*'[56]

In a missional context of constant and accelerating change, this is crucial. Institutions of any significant size, but certainly any size beyond which it is possible to listen to one another well, are pretty hopeless at adapting. They are utterly hopeless at adapting fast. This terrifies large successful organisations like Facebook and Google, who recognise that without constant innovation they are likely to be superseded by the latest digital start-up emerging from some unknown coder's bedroom. Their commitment and investment in innovation is absolutely crucial to their survival, to the extent that these organisations from the top to the bottom are looking to hard-wire the start-up mentality into every part of their organisation. This includes keeping staff levels low and (significantly) project teams tiny, with a high value for creative thinking.[57]

Of course, the great motivation for tech companies to adapt, be creative, etc. is in staying ahead in the innovation race – and that in turn is about survival, market-share and investor return. In the case of the church, our motivation shouldn't be about innovation for its own sake, but the attentiveness and receptibility to the Spirit, which is God's constant invitation and for which adaptability and innovation are a hallmark. Within the church, therefore, valuing the place of small communities is absolutely fundamental to the call we have to listen to the Spirit and adapt to the new thing he is leading us into. This has always been true. But it is absolutely critical in the ferociously fast-changing context in which we now live. Our overvaluing of the large and the busy church runs the risk of organising out a part of the church's fundamental nature: the disrupting, adaptive life of the Spirit. It also runs the risk of organising out our ability to listen deeply or quickly to the community around us, leaving to small numbers of overwhelmed leaders the task of responding to what the Spirit might be saying to the churches.

The missional community of which I am part could be described as a place in which the responsibility to listen to the Spirit, at work in each other and in the community around us, has been given back to the 'ordinary' membership of the community. We do not run projects or programmes. Instead, we seek to guard jealously the ethos of our community, which trusts the work of the Spirit in each of us and trusts the body of Christ as a whole to be the best way of listening out for the Spirit at work in the world. We invite people to listen to the Spirit's call on their lives, to make connections between this and what God appears to be doing in the wider community. When someone starts to make these connections and comes up with an idea, we invite them to gather with a couple more people from the community to see if this idea can come to fruition. There is no particular thematic or strategic plan to this. Consequently, what emerges is a wonderful and surprising array of initiatives – little communities built around things as diverse as beer-making, walking, felt-making and film, each one a place where there is the opportunity for part of our community to live out something of the gospel alongside others. And all this in a community which is still only 40 or so adults. When we hold open the space for 'ordinary' Christian disciples to listen to the Spirit and take responsibility for mission, the level of participation this engenders is phenomenal.

Surely this is part of the transforming nature of exile for Israel and for the church in our own context: to confront us with the shallowness and insipidness of lazy ritual and observance, and to call us to the richness of participation in the renewing work of the Spirit. We will most likely choose the safety of institution and routine over the wild innovation and unpredictability of the Holy Spirit. So it is context which forces our hand and unsettles us from our structures of comfort.

The curtailed end to the vision in the valley of dry bones is an invitation to the exiles in Babylon to cease their vain hopes of restoration, to convert from a contractual relationship with God whereby he might be called upon to carry out certain functions on their behalf, and instead embrace a life of attentive participation in the active presence of God's Holy Spirit. They are invited to write the fulfilment of this vision with their own lives. And the very genesis of the vision, the extraordinary epiphany experienced by Ezekiel, as an exiled prophet-priest within the exile community, swept up into the presence of the Spirit in the midst of the community's alienation, argues that this invitation was not for some future time, some imminent return; it is for now. Israel is being invited to embrace this wild, creative presence of God in the very midst of their experience of exile. They are being invited to do this with the only thing they have left – each other. Renewal will come about through Israel as community embodying the presence of God by his Spirit.

As already mentioned, exile brought about some of the most daring and creative theological developments in Israel's history. But it also brought about a hugely innovative and creative period in the story of Israel's communal expression of God's presence, a renaissance and recreation of the call on the people of God to incarnate the presence of God as a blessing for others. This is the continuation of the vision, the opening chapter in the story of its fulfilment, a story which today's church continues to seek to write. But are there clues, lessons and insights from Israel's life after exile for the church's witness and mission today? I think there are. And to this we will now direct our attention.

5

Home by another route

Therefore prophesy and say to them: 'This is what the Sovereign Lord says: My people, I am going to open your graves and bring you up from them; I will bring you back to the land of Israel. Then you, my people, will know that I am the Lord, when I open your graves and bring you up from them. I will put my Spirit in you and you will live, and I will settle you in your own land. Then you will know that I the Lord have spoken, and I have done it, declares the Lord.'
EZEKIEL 37:12–14

And having been warned in a dream not to go back to Herod, [the Magi] returned to their country by another route.
MATTHEW 2:12

For the past five years, the Swedish home furnishing store, IKEA, has carried out an extensive international survey on the subject of home. The annual 'Life at Home Report' explores an aspect of home life, how people are thinking, feeling and developing their relationship with and experience of home. Their 2016 report explored how the concept of home is changing. Drawn from a survey of 12,000 people in twelve cities across the world, the report described how home is not just a physical space, and nor is it simply the place we leave and return to each day. Increasingly, home is a fluid concept, particularly in the urban environment where other social spaces, social media and a changing work environment are extending 'home' into a variety of spaces. Forty-two per cent of people, for example, said they felt more at home outside their actual residence. The report referred to home as 'a never-ending journey' and concluded that 'to truly understand what makes home, we must view home as a never-ending, constantly changing idea'.[58]

Yet, while our experience of home may be changing, what *we believe* home to be is remarkably constant across a range of cultures. People see home as a place of safety, a place of peace and a place of belonging, where we are connected to those we are close to and who know us intimately. Home is less a physical space then a locus for psychological well-being:

> What I think makes something a home, are the psychological functions that it serves. It's a place where we can feel protected, a place where we can feel provided for, a place where we can feel loved, a place where we can feel connected to others. The things that make a house a home are the psychological senses, the emotional senses. That's what makes it a home.[59]

For exiles, home is a concept under scrutiny, open to challenge, yet also open to innovation and reimagination. The displacement of exile, and perhaps also that of many urban dwellers trying to create home in an overcrowded and fluid physical environment, means that home is not a given, but something requiring reflection, intention and creativity. For the exile, the traditional concept of home, the deep memory of home with all its psychological associations of peace, well-being, harmony and security, is a thing of almost mythical importance. Only by keeping alive the memory of home, and the possibility of return, can the exile find hope in their experience of displacement.

Home in Babylon

For Israel, home is not only a psychological concept, but also a theological one. The Hebrew word *shalom*, most often translated 'peace', is a multivalent word that goes some way towards conveying the spiritual, physical and relational harmony that Israel hoped for.

They increasingly came to see this exclusively associated with the land of Israel, and focused in particular on Jerusalem and the temple where God's presence resided.

Yet, in the early exilic writings, this traditional construct of 'home' begins to be challenged. Jeremiah writing to the exiles makes the radical suggestion that they should treat *Babylon* like home! His prophetic word to the exiles is to 'build houses and settle down; plant gardens and eat what they produce' (Jeremiah 29:5). They are invited to marry and have children. Most significantly, Jeremiah tells them to 'seek the peace and prosperity [i.e. *shalom*] of the city to which I have carried you into exile' (Jeremiah 29:7).

That command was a direct challenge to the many voices among Israel's leadership arguing that exile would be temporary. These same voices argued for a continuation of the traditional concept of home. What is so radical about Jeremiah's message is not just that it argues for a different political policy in response to the exile; more than that, his prophecy opens up a whole new concept of home, a whole new way of being the people of God. *Shalom* need not be the exclusive preserve of God's people in a particular place and a particular structure of life. The *shalom* of God could take a journey, relocate, and be reimagined and re-expressed even in the most hostile and inhospitable of places, the city of Babylon.

In the same way, Ezekiel's prophecy opens up a journey towards home, a home faithful to the deep principles of the call of God to his people, but yet a new kind of home, radically reimagined from the traditional home of the past.

The last section of the prophecy (Ezekiel 37:11–14) summarises and interprets the vision of the valley of dry bones. It affirms that this visible resuscitation of a destroyed army is more than simply a restoration; it is an act of resurrection. The vision which refers not simply to the military might of Israel but to 'the people of Israel' symbolises a people whose 'hope is gone', who are 'cut off'

(v. 11). But their salvation is more than a restoration of hope or a reconnection with the past; it is nothing less than a resurrection from the dead (v. 12). And, furthermore, this resurrection is bound up as one with the promise of the Spirit and the promise of homecoming (v. 14). There cannot be the one (resurrection) without the other (homecoming). This argues for a different kind of continuity with the concept of home than the hoped-for return to the land of Israel. The city of Jerusalem and the temple are finished. There is no going back in any real sense. The message of Ezekiel's prophecy is of 'a new future beyond the lost city'.[60] His message is of the possibility of hope and new life in a landscape beyond the ravages of the old one. Israel has passed through death and emerged into a new future that will have continuities with the old, but which is not just renewed but radically new. So this homecoming that God envisions through Ezekiel goes beyond the physical and political hopes of the exiles and many of those speaking on their behalf in what is left of Israel. This homecoming is theological – a new creation by God's Spirit of a way of being home as God's people in a host culture: a way of being home as a minority, as aliens, as tellers of a counternarrative: home as a faithful but reimagined way of being God's people again.

Home by another route

T.S. Eliot's poem 'The Journey of the Magi'[61] also explores this idea of homecoming, and the challenge of finding home in the light of a radically new intervention into the fabric of faith. The poem, written from the point of view of one of the magi, years after the event of Jesus' birth, creates a tough and unsentimental picture of the wise men's journey through hard weather and inhospitable places. The magi seem to feed off their lengthening memory of home, remembering 'the summer palaces on slopes, the terraces/And the silken girls bringing sherbet'. Years later, the narrator tries to come to terms with the impact that the journey and encounter had on him.

Were we led all that way for
Birth or Death? There was a Birth, certainly
We had evidence and no doubt. I had seen birth and death,
But had thought they were different; this Birth was
Hard and bitter agony for us, like Death, our death.
We returned to our places, these Kingdoms,
But no longer at ease here, in the old dispensation,
With an alien people clutching their gods.
I should be glad of another death.

The familiar physical encounter with birth and death were different to this encounter with Christ, which was both birth and yet somehow also death. There are continuities and discontinuities. The magi returned to their places, their homes, presumably their palaces with the silken girls and the sherbet (or were these nostalgic visions of a lost past?), yet they cannot be at home any more. They are 'no longer at ease... in the old dispensation' and see their home in a new light, their neighbours like 'alien people clutching their gods'. Nothing on the surface has changed, and yet this momentous journey of so many years ago changed everything. It gave, as Rowan Williams commenting on the poem said, 'a new perspective on everything and a new restlessness in a tired and chilly world'.[62]

When Matthew came to write his gospel, he chose to include the story of the wise men journeying to bring their worship to Jesus. Having seen Jesus and presented their gifts, Matthew tells us that they were warned in a dream not to return to the anxious and scheming Herod. Instead, he says, 'they returned to their country by another route' (Matthew 2:12). Yes, physically they went home a different way. But does Matthew also want to tell us something more profound – that these spiritual seekers from another land left changed, disoriented, blinded by wonder, their spiritual as well as navigatory senses disrupted, opened to new horizons and new possibilities? They returned to their country, their physical land, by another route, but in all other ways they were different. So it is with anyone, Matthew challenges his readers, that an encounter with

Jesus reorients and rewires us. We will no longer 'be at ease' and familiar dispensations will now seem 'old' in the light of the new spiritual landscape that has come.

This is also, I would argue, the summary message of the vision in the valley of dry bones. The conventionally anticipated route home has emphatically been barred by this vision. The house of Israel, in its old dispensation, is dead. Resuscitation is not an option. The only option is a resurrection by God's intervening and life-giving Holy Spirit. And such an intervention will bring this longed-for homecoming. There will be continuity. The people of Israel will once again live life in the growing light of *shalom*. However, the means of arriving at the vision of hope is 'by another route'. Home must be reimagined as a primarily spiritual and relational concept and the symbols, rituals and structures of home life must be reimagined faithfully, in partnership with the Holy Spirit. In this way, Israel will come home.

Cairns in the wilderness

In the same way, I believe that the church, looking for a way home in a cultural landscape that has lost the familiar paths and landmarks of the past, must also return 'by another route'. The way back has been cut off. Recreating Jerusalem in the landscape of Babylon is not an option. The structures and the consensus of Christendom have gone. Any vestiges of that era are like dry bones: memories of a significant and different time, a time which will not return. For many, that remains something to be contested. For others, it is something to lament, recognising the power of its reality but needing time to come to terms with the new dispensation. But for others still, it is already tinged with light from a new dawn of possibility, already replete with signs of a resurrection, a landscape that, with eyes to see, is even now populated with signs of the faithful reimagination of Christian communal life. The route home can only be made one stretch at a time. Like the vision of Ezekiel, it is being made by those prophets and pioneers who have ventured open-eyed and open-hearted into the contemporary valley of dry bones, come face-to-face with the reality of the end of Christendom, listened to the 'four winds' bringing life out of a barren landscape and offered themselves to nurture that life with others.

The emergent and renewed communities that result from the ministry of these modern Ezekiels are beginning to lay a path home. However, a new paradigm cannot be fully planned. We may not be able to restructure our way out of Babylon, but neither can we plot a new route based solely on the first few forays into the unknown. The way home cannot be made by replacing one set of structures for another. Instead, old structures must be surrendered and a new way of being explored by faith, through experiment, innovation, theological reflection, prayer and obedience to the Spirit. We will make this way by walking in it. There will be those pioneers who have the gift of seeing further than most can, and who in their experimentation make cairns, altars, way-markers in a disorientating landscape for others to follow. These individuals and the communities they lead must be listened to and valued for what they bring to whole church, for the information and innovation they offer for everyone. And in this way, stage by stage, cairn by cairn, milepost by milepost, we will make our way in the wilderness.

What emerges from the literature of the exile of Israel is a deep reflection and reappraisal of a similar process within the exiled communities in Babylon. The exilic literature is not a new manual for being God's people; it is the honest record of a people finding a new way. It features pioneers and prophets such as Ezekiel, Jeremiah, Daniel, Esther, Jonah and others who represent the beginnings of a road home. What they discover, through hard-fought and often painful experience, lays a trail for the rest of Israel to follow. Other writers of the exile reflect theologically on these experiences and so start to populate what we have received as the Old Testament with startlingly new insights into God and what it means to be his people. These writers include a priestly writer, known by scholars as 'P', who is the source of a significant portion of the Pentateuch and whose writings are now generally thought to have been edited into these books after the exile. They also include Deutero-Isaiah, the writer of the second section of the book of Isaiah, who is almost certainly writing in the post-exilic period. These writings offer a window into the new journey the people of Israel embarked on in exile, and offer us insight and encouragement in our own journey of faithful reimagination.

Looking at these writings as a whole, themes begin to emerge that express the way in which Israel creatively responded to the exile, both theologically and in terms of their practices and structures of communal life. These themes provide a lens through which we might evaluate and reflect on our own experience and expression of what it means to be the people of God in our own age. They are arenas of renewal, evidence of the renewing work of the Spirit in the life of Israel, which in many ways testify to a progressive movement in Jewish theology and life, but also represent a return to the fundamentals of God's covenant with them.

1 A renewed vision of God's presence

Exilic literature is hugely daring in questioning the limited assumptions of how and where God is present to Israel. Prior to the exile, the basis for Israel's understanding of the presence of God was formed by the land, the monarchy and the temple. Furthermore, the exile challenged the assumption that Yahweh was the one true God. Israel's defeat and the destruction of the key structures in which God's presence was mediated argued for the defeat of God himself and the collapse of the covenant altogether. But, instead of yielding to this threat, the exiles begin to chart a new territory that reclaims a vision for God as present in and sovereign over all things, including those in exile and the alien culture they found themselves in.

The opening vision of Ezekiel is a description of God which is wholly at odds with the conventional understanding of God's presence. Liberated from the temple, God's presence comes in the form of a storm from the north. The key feature of this vision is the movement of a structure 'like a wheel intersecting a wheel', all under the direction of the spirit (Ezekiel 1:4–21). The power and apocalyptic nature of the vision leave the reader overwhelmed with the impression of a God on the move – untameable, incomprehensible, beyond the limits of our descriptive abilities. The immediate implication of this is that God's presence and sovereignty are not restricted by land, monarchy and temple – 'Yahweh's glory… is present wherever he chooses to reveal it, including Babylon.'[63] Furthermore, the vision impresses on its readers that God's presence is not a commodity, a utility – he 'refuses to be useful'.[64] He cannot and will not be confined to the structures we may have constructed to organise his presence and power. Our institutions and our theologies must move and develop, and they must not imagine that they can ever contain a God who is by nature uncontainable.

In much the same way, the story of Jonah bursts wide open the borders of Israel's conception of God. This short story could be seen as a journey through various containers: Israel, the ship, the whale, the city of Nineveh and the booth that Jonah constructs for himself at the edge of the city. In each, God is present and active. He is unremittingly unrestricted, either by Israel's political and theological assumptions of him, Jonah's attempts to avoid him, the presence of pagans, the supposed spiritual vacuum of the sea or the chief enemy status of the Assyrians of Nineveh. 'I knew that you are a gracious and compassionate God' (Jonah 4:2), says an exasperated Jonah at the end, implying that he had no idea that this gracious nature of God extended beyond the borders of Israel or that it would follow him wherever he went.

To these examples we might also add the letter of Jeremiah, which has already been mentioned. The advice to 'seek the peace and prosperity of the city' can only be interpreted as an affirmation of the continued presence of God with his people. _Shalom_ as a concept cannot be severed from the person of God. 'Peace and prosperity' in the mind of Israel is not just a psychological or material experience;

it is a holistic reality, which can only be brought into being in relationship with God. Furthermore, this is the God who 'carried you into exile', who can be sought and found in exile, and will intervene to bring them out of exile (Jeremiah 29:7, 12–14).

I began my work as a pioneer minister in Poole by listening. I spent time in the local history museum, understanding the development of the town of Poole as well as its spiritual history, I talked to church leaders, local community leaders and councillors, and of course to local residents. I walked the streets, praying and listening until the character and personality of Poole began to take shape in my heart and mind. After about three months of doing this, I felt I needed to listen more deeply, in particular to the attitudes of people who didn't go to church. I asked about 30 people, in one-to-one interviews, about their experience of God and about the practices which enabled them to experience God, if indeed they did. It was a fascinating experience. I found that the majority of those I talked to had vibrant and significant experiences of God. They were not vague experiences, but on the whole experiences about which each individual spoke with conviction. Furthermore, I found that about half of those I talked to either prayed or meditated in order to get in touch with God. However, in asking people what support or input people might look for in furthering their experience of God, it was very clear that most people wanted to journey on their own terms. Books, websites and Facebook groups were often a part of people's quest, but rarely was an organised form of religion or spirituality something people seemed to seek out or want.

The results of my small research project surprised me in terms of the degree to which people were reporting spiritual experiences. However, it did not surprise me that people were engaging with God outside the structures and communities of the church. For years, while secularists have been predicting the demise of religion in the face of the dominance of materialist worldviews, people have continued to explore a spiritual dimension to life. They may not be flocking towards institutional forms of religion to carry out this quest, often opting for more private and individually directed approaches to their exploration, but that they are engaging with God as they understand him is evident.

It might be easy enough to dismiss this spiritual movement in the secular west, to argue perhaps that it is a move towards a kind of smorgasbord paganism rather than any meaningful search for God as the Christian church understands him. But if we hold that any meaningful quest for God can only be made within terms of our own making, and within structures of our control, we are protecting precisely the same utilitarian attitude to God that the exile and exilic writers challenged. Who says that God cannot be present in the uncertain and undirected spiritual pilgrimages of those trying to navigate the bewildering landscape of the post-Christendom west? And what might we be protecting in ourselves if we say that he can't? If God can be sought and found in Babylon, where all the conventional containers for his presence and power were thought to have been lost, he can surely be sought and found in the growing spiritual hinterlands of the west created by the demise of institutional religion.

Theologically speaking, the growing influence of the concept of *missio Dei* has given a firmer basis for a positive attitude to the presence of God among both people and communities in our secular culture. Put simply, the principle of *missio Dei* argues that it is God's very nature to be missional. Mission is not something that God does, but something that God *is*.[65] Furthermore, God is by his very nature present and active in people and places where his embodied presence, the church, is not. The church's task is not to assume the role of mission agency, as though if it didn't no mission would take place. Rather, it is to take the role of mission partner, participating in the mission of God in every context and every community.

The implications of this (re)discovery are as significant for the church as they were for Israel. Two implications in particular are most relevant. Firstly, the dominant understanding of mission as a centripetal, or 'in-gathering', process is brought into tension with a centrifugal, or 'venturing-out', process. Israel's mission as a nation called to bless other nations begins with a venturing-out, a journey into the unknown, a staged journey outwards and onwards, which would be guided and unfolded by God's revelation (Genesis 12:1–9). This posture for mission, an attitude that is nomadic and attentive, becomes lost as Israel settled in the promised land and as the institutions of monarchy and priesthood developed. The centrifugal dimension of mission is kept alive in the realm of the prophetic, but bursts back into the mainstream during the exile. The word of God through Jeremiah to seek *shalom* in Babylon reaffirms this lost dimension of the mission of the people of God.

Likewise, the end of Christendom is renewing the centrifugal partner in the dynamic of God's mission for the western church in particular. Our comfort and complacency as an established presence in our communities, to which people simply come by virtue of birth or to be served at key transitional moments of life and death, has to be challenged by the new landscape around us. This is a landscape still populated by the visible symbols of Christendom, churches, chapels, cathedrals and the like, but where the power and relevance of those symbols is diminishing fast. We can take the approach of trying to keep the centripetal attraction of our established churches as potent as it was, but the forces around us will increasingly mitigate against this. Like Israel, we are being invited back to a mode of mission that ventures out. However, we do so on the understanding that we are not venturing out into the complete unknown. God is present in the Babylon of our own culture. He is present and active among the increasing proportion of people who have little or no connection with the Christian heritage of the past. We are being invited to join with God in seeking his *shalom* alongside them.

Secondly, the mission of God, *in dialogue with* the embodied life of God, becomes the organising principle around which the church orients. As Israel discovered, the dangers of a settled existence lay in creating the kind of established structures that ended up domesticating God, limiting his presence and power within the institutions that were intended to facilitate those same things. Israel became oriented around one particular way of expressing the call of being God's people, with his presence central to their communal life. They idolised this particular way of being the people of God as the only way of expressing that calling – the tradition of the covenant ossified into an introspective traditionalism which ultimately cost them everything.

In the same way, the relationship between the church and the world around it must be open to adaptation. One particular established way of being the church must not be confused with some sort of eternal divine ordinance. Christendom cannot be confused with Christianity or the kingdom of God. 'Christendom is no more than a phase in the history of Christianity, and it represents only one of many possible relationships between church and society.'[66] It is therefore in recovering the missional dimension of the church, *in dialogue with* the call on the church to embody the presence of God in community, that the church can orient its life and structures in creative and adaptive ways. As Alan Hirsch said, 'When the church engages with the fringes it almost always brings life to the centre.'[67] But, of course, it is not that the church engages in mission *so that* it can renew its central life. Communal life and mission are dialogue partners because they are twin expressions of the nature of God, who is both community and *missio Dei*, a missionary presence in the world. Only when the church expresses both is it truly being what it is called to be.

2 A renewed vision of holiness

In a similar way, the call on God's people to be a holy people received a renewed and reimagined call in the literature of the exile. The threat posed to the exiled community is of the loss of identity. The traditional symbols of identity, and the ritualistic purifying functions that they enabled, have been destroyed, so the community in exile was faced with the challenge of how to express holiness in this new context. And in this context, holiness becomes more than religious observance; it becomes a way of asserting minority identity within a hostile and dominant society.

The need to assert identity in conditions of exile are what Smith-Christopher in his study of other exiled communities called 'rituals of survival'.[68] The exilic literature sees the reassertion of key rituals of the covenant as way of ensuring that an identity as the holy people of God is preserved. It is now generally thought, for example, that the holiness codes of Leviticus 17—26 were shaped into their established form in the time of the exile. This body of material, with its rules of both restraint and positive behaviour, with the repeated appeal to relationship with Yahweh (the phrase 'I am the Lord your God' occurs some 22 times within these chapters), sheds light on a community working hard to assert its identity in an alien culture.

Smith-Christopher also argues that it is not so much the shaping of these rules into a definitive text that is revealing, but that they are reinterpretations of older traditions. He singles out the Hebrew word *badal* (to distinguish or separate) in the holiness code as 'a key term in the post-exilic concept of a separated and pure people'.[69] In other words, what is taking place is a shift in the way that holiness rituals are perceived and practised. They are now practised assertively as a means of preserving identity and ensuring survival as a people. Circumcision as a tradition likewise takes on a greater significance in the exile and becomes a 'rich and larger metaphor for faith'[70] with, for example, the call to 'circumcise your hearts' (Deuteronomy 10:16; 30:6, Jeremiah 4:4). Sabbath-keeping becomes a central act of faith and survival, an assertion that the Hebrew people 'refuse[d] to be defined by the production system of Babylon, so that life is regularly and with discipline enacted as a trusted gift and not as frantic achievement'.[71] What I would argue we see is Israel beginning to rediscover the covenant behind the commandments; that beyond the call to purity is a call to obedience and commitment to Yahweh in whatever circumstances they find themselves. Beyond the commandment of circumcision is a call to offer their whole selves as a people set apart for God. Beyond the commandment to keep the sabbath is a call to trust the God of all creation and all time.

Kenneth Bailey, in his interpretation of the story of the prodigal son, argues that Jesus is reinterpreting the story of Jacob and Esau (see Genesis 27:1—36:8; Luke 15:11–32).[72] This too is a story of exile and return, with the prodigal son's journey and homecoming, playing out the story of Jacob's exile to Haran and his anxious return. In both, the exile returns expecting the punishment that would be the anticipated results of his actions. In both, the material consequences are not meted out and there is a reconciliation of relationship. Jesus, reworking this story for his audience of purity-oriented Pharisees, is driving home the point that sin is not primarily a material or even ethical issue, and it is not fundamentally about cleanliness or codes of behaviour; it is about relationship. Holiness is a relational concept. And what God is eternally interested in is restoring that relationship for us and in us, for in doing so the issues of ethics and purity will begin to sort themselves. This is precisely what we begin to see emerging from the exile: the rediscovery of ritual and communal practice as a means to an end rather than an end in itself – a means of living out in daily life a critical relationship with Yahweh, the God of Israel.

The church, similarly, living in a culture no longer shaped by the values and ethics that develop from a relationship with God through Christ, must ask what our stance is as a minority community. There are those that argue that the secular culture we now inhabit is something to withdraw from. Our best hope is to live out our Christian faith quietly with as little relationship with our culture as possible, waiting for the judgement and the vindication of our obedience. This equates closely to those at the exile who advocated such a position in Babylon and for whom the expected restoration, through the miraculous intervention of God, corresponded to that same hope of vindication. There are those who believe that culture should be won for Christ, and for whom the way to achieve this is to create Christian expressions of cultural elements, a Christian subculture of literature, media, schools, alongside yet at a distance from mainstream culture. But the testimony of the exile argues for something different. It argues for a positive engagement as a minority with the dominant culture in ways that connect with it, partner with it, challenge it and live in dialogue with it, while at all times maintaining a primacy of allegiance and commitment to Christ.

In such an engaged, open and missional stance within secular culture, the challenge of the church is, I believe, to live authentically Christian communal lives of attractive distinctiveness. It is undoubtedly true that this will entail some significant distinctives in terms of our worldview, what we fundamentally believe about God and about the world we live in. However, in terms of our positive engagement with culture, in seeking the 'peace and prosperity of the city to which I have called you', we must do what Israel did in exile and take seriously rituals and patterns of practice in our individual and communal lives.

Our community in Poole, Reconnect, has been exploring and experimenting with this for some years now. As a missional community, we founded our identity on a 'way of life', a series of statements that sought to set out in practical terms the way we felt called to live out the gospel as a community.[73] We were conscious that many of these statements were challenges to the values at work in our own society, values such as materialism, consumerism and individualism. So, we hoped and prayed that, in living out these values ourselves, we would be living out a distinctive expression of the Christian faith that some, particularly those questioning the values of our culture, would find provocative and attractive. We have found, as we have drawn others into the fringes of our community, that this way of asserting our distinctiveness, our holiness as a Christian community, as a positive orthopraxy (right living) in society, is a truly life-giving experience. It creates space for others who do not hold the same beliefs, or who cannot affirm a relationship with Christ, to belong with us – and, critically, for us to belong with them.

It means we can journey together with others also beginning to explore fullness of life, lives oriented around service and sacrifice, justice for the poor and the environment, but who (as yet) have not committed themselves to follow Jesus, the source of that life.

Similarly, in the work I have done engaging with the workplace, we have used practices that embody a countercultural way of living as a way of connecting with others. My experience of listening to people's spiritual experiences convinced me that we needed to venture out to meet people on their journey. At the same time, in a town centre with a number of large places of employment present, I wanted to see how we might connect with people at their place of work. So we began offering stilling exercises and contemplative prayer in some of these workplaces. In each place, a group of about ten to twelve people gathered at lunchtime and enjoyed half an hour of quiet, which included an invitation to meditate on a short piece of scripture.

One of the questions I have found it helpful to ask when looking to connect with a context is: what might be the good news here? How does the story of the gospel engage with the story of this context? In other words, how might the transforming life of the gospel make an initial connection here? In those lunchtime groups, I think the answer was that we were inviting people to experience sabbath. We were modelling sabbath, which, as the exiles discovered, is not just the command to rest, but an invitation to realign ourselves and to commit ourselves in trust to the God of time. Sabbath is a pause not simply for recuperation, but for critical reflection on our desires and drivers.

> Sabbath is a school for desires, an exposé and critique of the false desires that focus on idolatry and greed and have immense power for us. When we do not pause for sabbath, the false desires take over us. But sabbath is the chance for self-embrace of our true identity.[74]

We were offering sabbath not just as a tool for recovery, a means of making it through the day, but as an alternative to the relentless system of achievement, accomplishment and performance. We were offering a glimpse of an alternative way of life, one not predicated on achievement or acquisition but on faith in the sovereignty of God. The connection from the world of work to the world of faith was a practice, a spiritual discipline of stopping, stilling and being attentive. In this and other ways, the life-giving practices of holiness, expressions of our primary relationship with God, can become provocative means of proclaiming an alternative identity and way of life in the midst of a culture aligned towards other gods.

3 A renewed vision of engagement with the world

As already mentioned, the reality of exile was to Israel a challenge to the very nature of God's relationship with them. 'The greatest threat to the exiles is the power of despair'[75] formed by doubt over God's willingness to intervene and save them or indeed his capacity to do so. The triumph of power over the symbols and structures of faith has cast doubt on the validity of God and his covenant relationship with Israel. Israel struggles to imagine what possible renewal of covenant faith there can possibly be in this situation in which the only options appear to be the abandonment of faith or a retreat into private religion and a practical assimilation into their host culture. The exilic literature, however, begins to show new routes of hope and imagination in terms of how Israel begins to conceive of its relationship with the world.

One key element of this reimagination is the renewal of community as a locus for covenant faithfulness. This theme can be perceived emerging in a number of places but in particular in the final section of Deutero-Isaiah. This body of prophecy returns Israel to its original call to be a blessing to others (Genesis 12:3) and a priestly nation whose call is to enable the flourishing of the lives of others (Exodus 19:6). The key voice in this prophetic message is that of the suffering servant. The four 'servant songs' (Isaiah 42:1–9;

49:1-6; 50:4-10; 52:13—53:12) create a new landscape for Israel in which vulnerability, suffering and service will exemplify a renewed posture of blessing towards the other nations of the world. This is a completely new paradigm in contrast to the pre-exilic status quo, which is characterised by a militarism, exclusivism and territorialism which was hardly distinguishable from the surrounding nations.

It is not just a renewed commitment to a posture of blessing that is distinctive, however. The servant songs invite a communal reading that encourages Israel, as a community, to embrace this new vision. The identity of the suffering servant in these songs is a subject of fierce scholarly debate. Yet, reading them as invitations to the whole community to embrace the ministry of the servant is not without warrant. 'The national community is spoken of in terms of an individual, as is often the case in the Bible.'[76] In which case, Isaiah may well be using the motif of the anointed individual to invite all of Israel to reimagine itself as carrying the call and anointing to bring blessing to others. This flow can be identified, for example, in the famous passage from Isaiah 61 which describes the anointing of an individual (61:1), and a call to renew the fortunes of the exiles (61:2-3) in order that they might take up this call to be bearers of righteousness and renewal (61:3-4). Of course, this passage is then taken up by Jesus when he announces his own ministry of spiritual renewal. Having announced his public ministry with this passage, he forms a community that can embody, share and ultimately continue that same ministry (Luke 4—5).

This reading of the servant songs is also consistent with the theme of participation that emanates from much of the exilic literature. As we have already explored, the form of Ezekiel's vision invites participation and it is therefore highly likely that Ezekiel's participation in the vision of the valley of dry bones models the kind of communal participation in the renewal of covenant faithfulness that God was inviting Israel into. There is an open-endedness in the exilic literature, a consistent questioning, which is not rhetorical, but designed to invite all of Israel into a response.

I am led to conclude from this that in exile Israel experienced a renewal of community as the locus for its engagement with the world, an engagement which was based on servanthood and humility rather than on dominion and power. It is this renewed focus on community that offers the church in the secular west another element of hope in its search for a way home. Institutions can no longer represent faith in the same way that they once did; they cannot act as a convenient shorthand for faithful living or authentic Christianity. They have been devalued and discredited in our culture, to the extent that no amount of rebranding or restructuring can fix. It is the experience of faith lived in community, in the daily practice and rhythm of people's lives that speaks most clearly and authentically to the culture in which we live. As Lesslie Newbigin argued:

> How is it possible that the gospel should be credible, that people should come to believe the power which has the last word in human affairs is represented by a man hanging on a cross? I am suggesting that the only answer, the only hermeneutic of the gospel, is a congregation of men and women who believe it and live by it.[77]

It is worth adding, however, that a 'congregation' can be a very different thing to a 'community'. To be credible expressions of the Christian faith in a culture weary and sceptical towards organised religion and deeply distrusting of institutions, we need authentic communal expression of faith, not simply collections of people who come together from time to time to do the same things and affirm the same beliefs. This requires us to think firstly how the relationships we have with one another communicate the gospel, and secondly how our communal expression of faith presents a posture of openness, vulnerability and servanthood to the world around us. Organised faith all too easily slips into the client–provider mode of engagement with the world, where the church can remain in a position of relative power among those it serves. All too often, this simply creates two kinds of congregation, one on one side of a counter or desk, and one on another. But to serve as exiles is to serve from a position of humility and vulnerability. It is to say that we have as much to receive as to give; to say that we have as much to learn as we might begin to think we have to teach; to say that community is something none us have a monopoly on and that is always open to the gifts of others.

This theme is picked up strongly in another strand of exilic literature, that of the 'diaspora advice tale'. This genre, which includes the books of Esther, Daniel and Jonah, was a means of responding to exile and engaging with the new context, in ways that could be reflected on and explored. In each, the individual hero of the story comes to symbolise Israel and, in so doing, offers a rich resource for reflection for the exiles working out how to live faithful lives in such a radically different context. These stories, when compared, show some clear similarities – the appointment of an individual into a pagan (often court) setting, the presentation of a task or challenge which threatens the life of the hero, the (often miraculous) overcoming of this challenge, followed by the restoration of the hero to a position higher than before. These tales gave hope to the exiles. They said, for example:

> One could, as a Jew, overcome adversity and find a life both rewarding and creative within a pagan setting and as part of this foreign world; he need not cut himself off from that world or seek hope for its destruction.[78]

But it is not just what happens but the way it happens that is also informative. The hero is invariably an unlikely candidate for hero status, sometimes from a humble background, sometimes exhibiting deficiencies of character. The hero does not impose him/herself on the situation; the mode of success is very often one of patience, wisdom, even cunning. The focus is on the obedience and faithfulness of the hero more than their abilities. Even where (in the case of Jonah) their obedience in questionable, nevertheless the narrative is inviting the reader to reflect on their own obedience and seek greater commitment. Finally, the eventual triumph of the hero is a result of prayer, the intervention of God, the interpretation of a dream, and results invariably in benefits for the exiles *and those they live among*.

These tales affirm a conviction that a communal posture of quiet, insistent, prayerful and humble service as a minority community, in the midst of a dominant culture, is what we are called to as exiles in the secular west. These stories advocate a rejection of aggressive, adversarial or domineering approaches to engagement with the wider world. They were a rejection of the modes of engagement that had clearly failed them, and of which exile was the dramatic result. The renewal of the people of Israel was intimately bound up with this renewed posture, this renewed call to be a blessing to the other nations of the world. Hence, renewal is not an exclusive pursuit for the church. Instead, it is united with our call to 'seek the peace and prosperity of the city into which I have carried you into exile… *because if it prospers, you too will prosper*' (Jeremiah 29:7, italics mine).

All of this begs the question of what our motives for renewal and reform are in our own age. The inordinate amount of attention given to church growth does not sit well with a posture of servanthood that has the renewal of all things at its heart. We might argue that growth is necessary if we are going to have a capacity to serve our wider world. But that seems a category error in the light of our study of the Jewish exiles. Here, the call to renewal is a call back to the first principle being a blessing to the nations: 'My life and death are with my neighbour,' as the desert fathers put it.[79] We are not called to growth but to faithfulness, to be a blessing to others, to be communities that live out and hold out that life of blessing faithfully and consistently.

We may well be coming to terms with being a small church, of being more like David than Goliath, but our attention to the metrics and strategies of growth belie a hope that perhaps, after all, being David is just a phase – a temporary aberration in the order of things.

After all, doesn't David vanquish Goliath and end up exalted to the monarchy? Doesn't the runt end up a ruler? Isn't that what the story means? No; exile asks us to relinquish our status more than just temporarily. It asks us to relinquish the very paradigm in which being Goliath was ever, or could ever, be thought of being a good thing. Exile invites the rejection of power, coercion, domination, aggression and the myth of redemptive violence. Exile invites us to embrace positively a new way of being that is permanently more like David and, even further, a way of being in which Goliath is not someone to be conquered or dominated, but someone we will always likely live alongside.

Exile invites us to live in the shadow of Goliath, as small communities in the context of Babylon, faithfully and without fear. Our focus is not the downfall of the system but the nurturing of dissident communities of life, characterised by the presence of God, the authentic expression of gospel-oriented lives and an attitude of open-hearted servanthood to those around us.

6

Beyond exile: a new story 'from below'

I will put my Spirit in you and you will live, and I will settle you in your own land. Then you will know that I the Lord have spoken, and I have done it, declares the Lord.
EZEKIEL 37:14

Since the news came of the death of American evangelist Billy Graham, tributes have poured in and many stories have been recalled from people's experience of his rallies in the UK. Some of the media's reflections on his life made sure to point out that, after becoming a Christian in his late teens, Billy nearly went into sales and marketing, until eventually deciding to go to Bible college. When he came to the UK in 1955, the use of advertising to publicise his rallies caused much debate. Similarly, the use of rousing music at the point of the altar call lent many to see his success as merely a result of American-style marketing and emotionalism. When he returned to the UK in 1966, Billy Graham responded to these accusations and instructed the choir that they should only sing the famous altar call hymn, 'Just as I am', if directed to by him. In the end, Billy Graham preached for 30 nights that year, and 'Just as I am' was never sung. People remember a great silence after the altar call lasting what seemed like an age, before the sound was heard of a squeaking of a seat, and then another, and another, until hundreds of people began getting up and walking to the front. The press wrote that all they heard was the shuffling of feet on the floor and said, 'Bring back "Just as I am"! The silence is killing us!'[80] In 1991, he came to Murrayfield in Scotland. My wife Emily was part of the team of counsellors who supported the rally. She remembers, every night, wondering if anyone was going to come forward at the altar call. The message seemed so simple, so lacking in elaboration, so straightforward. Yet, time after time, when Billy Graham made the altar call and stepped back from the microphone, people streamed forward.

What is clear to those who knew Billy Graham, and those who supported his rallies from churches up and down the country, is that his appeal was not based on the advertising or the music or the power of his own words, but on the power of the gospel and the Holy Spirit's power to convince and convict. 'We are not going to have any music tonight,' he said at Earl's Court in 1966, 'there'll be no singing. But if the Spirit of God is speaking to your heart, then right where you are, just stand in your place, and make your way out to the aisle.'[81] He ministered under the conviction this his role was to participate in a move of God's Spirit that he had been graciously invited into. Like Ezekiel in the valley of dry bones, he was obedient to what he was asked to do, but recognised that he was partnering with a sovereign and powerful God. His job was to preach the gospel in the language, idioms and forms the people of his generation could understand. And then it was to get out of the way and allow God, by his Spirit, to do the rest.

The vision of Ezekiel 37 is a charismatic vision. It begins and ends with the Spirit, and the presence of the Spirit saturates every part of the text. The Hebrew word *ruach*, translated variously as 'spirit', 'wind', 'breath', occurs ten times in a space of 14 verses. God's Spirit is the initiator of the vision (v. 1), the result of the vision (v. 14) and the key transformative agent in the pivotal moment in the vision as the resuscitated army are reanimated by the breath of God (v. 10). It is perhaps worth reflecting that, while the Spirit is the beginning and the end and is the main actor in the whole scene, he is also something of a mysterious, elusive player. The language of the Spirit itself is playful and indistinct, multivalent and oblique, as though the Spirit will not dominate. The Spirit comes as breath and wind, as noun and verb ('breath… breathe', v. 9). The Spirit is revealed in symbol but seems to hide from pronouns, from being tied down too definitely, lest he be objectified and controlled.

The presence of the Spirit in these verses is more than just an explanation of the mechanics of resurrection; rather, it is a window into the kind of renewed community God is calling Israel to be. The climax of this comes in verse 14. Firstly, 'I will put my Spirit in you and you will live.' Israel will experience what this dead collection of bones has experienced: the indwelling of the Spirit and the return of life. The Spirit will come to dwell within them and become a life-giving presence among them. God's presence among them, not merely mediated through the priesthood, the anointed monarchy and the temple, would define the nature of their life as a community. Secondly, as a result of this, 'You will know that I the Lord have spoken, and I have done it.' The work of the Spirit brings a conscious acceptance of the revelation and action of God and a surrender to the primacy of God's words and God's action over and above our own. God is concerned for the fate of the people of Israel in exile, but his ultimate concern is that Israel would return to a primal reliance on his words and his power to act. And between these spiritual consequences of God's promised intervention is the reality of homecoming. This is Israel's great yearning and hope, and it will be fulfilled: 'I will settle you in your own land,' the Lord declares. However, this longed-for homecoming, this return to their own settled existence and self-governance, is only relevant in the context of the deeper work of returning his people into surrendered relationship with him.

For the church in its search for home, its own quest for renewal, these final conclusions are key. The deeper invitation God makes is for the refounding of the church on fundamental reliance on his Holy Spirit and the pre-eminence of his word and action. While Israel's focus was on homecoming, God's invitation was for a renewal of their focus on him. Likewise, all our efforts at refounding, renewal, reform will be nothing unless they are built on a renewal of our reliance on God himself. This is hard for us to do, as hard as it was for Israel, when the weight and complexity of our forms and structures, the demands of our internal culture, constantly call for our attention and our concern. However, there are important insights here, which invite our attention in the midst of our own crisis as the church in the west. I will focus on the key areas of leadership and church organisation.

Leadership in the Spirit

The leadership model that develops in this passage begins with surrender, with the key words 'Sovereign Lord, you alone know' (v. 3). Leadership in exile is leadership without the structures and institutions that foster reliance. Leadership in exile invites a *revealed* knowledge rather than a *received* knowledge. Exile brings Israel back to reliance on a way forward based on episodes of revelation. The vision of Ezekiel 37 unfolds stage by stage, word by word, action by action; there is no blueprint or masterplan, even if that were one provided by God. This kind of leadership invites the leader to remain the seeker of limited knowledge: the guardian of the next step, not the whole journey.

Consequently, the main task of the leader will not primarily be one of strategy or organisation, but firstly being attentive to the Spirit, and secondly nurturing the kind of environments where others can be attentive to the same Spirit. This seems to be a very different kind of role to the one many ordained leaders in today's church find themselves yoked to – and quite possibly a very different role to the one many training colleges prepare people for. We may therefore be quite a long way off a church where the normative mode of leadership is one where the main agent of the church's life is not the leader but the Holy Spirit. Nevertheless, leadership matters and the kind of leadership that makes space for the Holy Spirit is key for our own renewal. This kind of leadership I believe is played out in two related spheres, the personal and the communal.

The attentive leader will make the practice of attending to the Spirit a priority in his/her life. Graham Cray suggests that there are four factors that affect a person's ability to listen to and discern the Spirit: worldview, charism (i.e. gifts of the Spirit), character and experience.[82] We lead on the understanding that the Spirit is present in our community. We can ask God for the gift of discernment. We can also develop practices that shape our character and experience in the realm of being attentive to and discerning the work of the Spirit.

The spiritual disciplines are the fruits of the generations of Christian leaders and other saints, showing us how we can grow in Christ, and how it is possible. In this area of discernment, the rich resource of spiritual practice around silence and contemplation is a gift to the leader seeking to grow in attentiveness to the Spirit. Rowan Williams has described prayer as being like the patient birdwatcher waiting to see the kingfisher.[83] There is no guarantee of seeing that flash of brilliant azure blue. Instead, prayer is about waiting and watching, committing oneself to the right attitude, posture and state of awareness that makes a glimpse of the kingfisher a real possibility.

And so the ground for such glimpses is solitude and silence, the daily discipline of coming without agenda or anxiety into the presence of God; coming such that he might have the first word, lest we crowd him out with all our strategic or organisational concerns. Above all, this is about maintaining a discipline that embodies the theology that 'the Spirit is not the church's auxiliary',[84] nor ours. It seeks to practise the reality that we are the auxiliaries, servants and junior partners in the work of the Spirit. Leadership in the church will constantly tempt us to believe otherwise. Our congregation and communities all too often collude with us to think we are vastly more important and influential than we really are. The humble, unnervingly simple practice of silence before God is an act of faith in the truth that we are not indispensable and only the Spirit is.

The practice of silent attentiveness in our personal spiritual lives feeds into our leadership in the communal sphere. Leadership in the Spirit invites a facilitative leadership that is above all concerned with creating the kind of spaces where others can experience and participate in the life of the Spirit. We model for others what the grace of God models for us, and create a participative environment that gives us freedom to act as valued agents in the ongoing work of God's Spirit. Furthermore, our task is to learn together, as a community, how to discern the work of the Spirit among us – which means that the leader must be open to discerning the gifts of others and encouraging of them, since it is the discerning ability of the whole community that is treasured, not just that of the leader.

Graham Tomlin, in his exploration of priesthood, argues for a 'priestly-leadership' which is consistently focused on enabling others to flourish and participate in the life of the kingdom. He takes as his starting point the principle of vocation as a call to bless, that the call of God on all people is a call to bless others. This call then radiates out like a series of ever-widening circles with Jesus at the centre. Thus, the priesthood are those called to be a blessing to the people of God (the church), Israel/the church is called to bless humanity (Genesis 12:1–3; Exodus 19:6; 1 Peter 2:9), humanity is called to bless creation (Genesis 1:28; 2:15).

> Priests in the church are called to enable the church to play its priestly role of declaring the praises of Jesus Christ, the true High Priest, so that in turn the rest of humanity might be restored to its proper priestly dignity, and the whole earth resound to the joy of God.[85]

Tomlin points out that priesthood is not an exclusive role, arguing for an inclusive priesthood of all believers that makes the call to priesthood universal by virtue of baptism. Priesthood is a call to leadership, a 'priestly-leadership' which is a participation in the priestly ministry of Christ, playing a facilitative role in Christ's desire to present the church as perfect offering to the Father.

Drawing on the early church father Basil the Great's writing on priesthood, Tomlin then draws out two key metaphors for 'priestly-leadership': the garden and the family. The priestly leader is like a gardener who puts in place all the right conditions for growth and works with the context and the resources at hand to enable a garden to flourish. Likewise, the priestly leader is like a parent who knows that domination or authoritarianism will not enable the flourishing of their children. Rather, encouragement, direction, advice and trust will create the kind of space in which children learn, grow and flourish.

These descriptions of leadership reflect the kind of leadership the church needs if it is to be a charismatic community, not in the narrow sense of whether or not we nurture particular gifts of the Spirit, but in terms of the call on the church to discern where the Spirit is at work in order to participate. We have been preoccupied, and still are in some cases, with the Spirit as a gift of power, when our first call is to see the Spirit as a gift of sight, helping to see and discern what the Spirit is doing so we might better be able to join in. Leaders of such a charismatic community need therefore to be much less central figures and much more peripheral, having a posture of humility and service, a desire to see their community flourish in its ability to hear God and participate in what he invites us to do. To invoke another metaphor, such a leader's role inhabits the sidelines much more than it does the pitch, rejoicing in the participation of others, constantly observing with a vigilance bent on shaping the players to play with even more God-inspired freedom and life.

Organising in the Spirit

A clear theme of the exilic literature is the liberation from institutional modes of organising life to more communal and democratised modes. Communal life needs forms of some kind. The question is which form is most able to give space for the presence and leading of the Holy Spirit. I believe that in the same way that exile for Israel brought about renewal of the forms of Jewish life, so for the church there are signs of a reforming of the church by the power of the Spirit in an age of huge cultural change. These changes are predominantly emergent in character, outpacing, in my opinion, all the best efforts of church institutions to adapt and reform in response to a changing world. Jürgen Moltmann describes it thus:

> We are living in the exciting era in which the Constantinian form of the church is slowly coming to an end and something new is being pioneered. This new form is coming from below – from men and women who are saying, 'We are the church!'[86]

Moltmann identifies three paradigms of church since the Constantinian age and the beginnings of Christendom. Firstly, the 'hierarchical paradigm' characterised by the Catholic Church in the Roman–Byzantine era, a church organised on the principle of holy rule with 'one God, one bishop, one church' and with an emphasis on God as Father. Secondly, the 'Christocentric paradigm' characterised by the Reformation's assertion of the 'priesthood of all believers' which organised itself through 'the synods of the congregations' with Christ, the emphasis and the head of the church. According to Moltmann's thesis, we are entering the 'charismatic paradigm', where the emphasis is on the Holy Spirit, where the gifts of the Holy Spirit are able to flourish and where the organisation of the church looks more like the fluid emergent forms of the New Testament church.

> In the charismatic congregation Christians come of age, and acquire the courage to live out their own experience of faith and to bring themselves with their own powers into the community of the coming of the kingdom of God.[87]

Others, too, have discerned epochal shifts in the forms of church in response to rapid changes in culture. Phyllis Tickle refers to our own experience of change and crisis as yet another 'semi-millennial rummage sale of ideas', one in a series of transitions that invites us to 'remove all of the old treasures that belonged to one's parents so as to get on with the business of keeping the house the new way'.[88] Tickle gives our own era the title 'The Great Emergence', arguing that the key locus for authenticity lies no longer in any particular structure but in local Christian communities and networks wrestling with the questions of faithfulness and authenticity. Likewise, Harvey Cox argues that we are entering the 'Age of the Spirit', evidence of which can be clearly seen in particular in the liberation theology movement, the Pentecostal movement and the emergent church/ pioneer ministry movement, all of which we might note are movements 'from below'.[89]

Institutions do not have a great history of welcoming the new forms and expressions of church that emerge from their fringes. The Celts, Lollards, Moravians, Anabaptists, Methodists and house churches have all either been suppressed, expelled or compelled to find their place outside the structures of established church. Furthermore, the dilemma of bringing form to a movement that is emergent and ground-up is in the danger of organising the very life out of it. Emergence must be given space in which to experiment and innovate without succumbing to the temptation to control by standardising, or institutionalising forms which are still in development.

However, one case study might be a good example of making space for the emergent reforming work of the Spirit. The Franciscan movement posed a radical and subversive challenge to the Catholic Church. St Francis' commitment to poverty, simplicity and a preference for the poor was an embodied critique of the power and wealth of the institution. Yet, as the movement began to grow, Francis journeyed from Assisi to Rome to seek the blessing of the pope and received it. This blessing is remarkable on two counts: that the pope was willing to give it, and that Francis both sought it and accepted it. It suggests that both were willing to keep the bonds of *relationship* in order to maintain space within an imperfect institution for this work of the Spirit to take shape. It argues that organising in the Spirit should in fact be less about organisation and more about relationship and communication.

Likewise, the Church Mission Society (CMS), founded by William Wilberforce, John Venn and others in 1799, also sought approval from church authorities to start its work. However, the Archbishop of Canterbury took 16 months to respond to their request and when it came it can only be described as neutral. No formal approval was given to the new society until 1805. The society also struggled to find British clergy to come forward as missionaries. Its first two missionaries were German Lutherans who sailed for Freetown, west Africa in 1804. Yet despite these marginalised beginnings, CMS succeeded in establishing Christian communities in much of Africa and the east, the results of which constitute much of what is the Anglican Communion today.[90] Today, CMS continues to provide a different kind of space, in relationship to the core institution, for new ventures of the Holy Spirit as host to a growing ministry of training and support for pioneers to the post-Christian society of the UK.[91]

Bishop Stephen Cottrell has said repeatedly that the parish system did not evangelise the British Isles, arguing that 'the parish system is the consequence of mission, not its cause'.[92] The Spirit leads us into the mission of God. Forms can come later. What is important if we are to keep making space for the Spirit, keep curating the kind of environments that nurture the innovating work of the Spirit, is that pioneers, prophets like Francis and those in positions of authority, keep a relationship of faith with each other and the work of the Spirit to which they are both committed.

There is one area in today's church in which this tension – between the established church and emergent movement that the Spirit is generating – seems more acute than anywhere else, and that is vocations. When someone senses a call to leadership, they will articulate the sense that the Spirit is at work in them. When the church comes to journey with and nurture that vocation, it has become the guardian of a precious thing, the work of God in an individual.

But I want to argue further that, in welcoming a person to explore their vocation in the church, the church is also being given the opportunity to listen to the kind of church God is building for the future. I always remember one of my tutors at training college warning us not to find ourselves 'turning the crank of the ecclesial machine'. Yet, nearly 15 years later, many of us are. And of those I trained with at college, a number are no longer in ministry, worn out and disillusioned by a vocation that seemed to offer a chance to lead in the church's mission, but which too often drew them into ecclesiastical managerialism. More recently, I talk to those articulating a call to pioneering who fear they are being domesticated by a church that doesn't seem able to find the space for them to explore a call to innovate and ends up squeezing them into standard roles instead. This is not an easy dilemma to resolve. Moltmann's three paradigms of church are not linearly sequential; all of them coexist to some extent. The new must negotiate for space among the continuing life of the old.

However, we too often listen like automated translation programmes to those bringing their half-formed articulations of their vocations. There are only a certain number of terms programmed into our vocabulary, we say, so whatever this person is trying to say must be one of them. Instead, we must allow those feeling a call to commissioned or ordained leadership from the liminal edges of the church to teach us new language. It will not be an unknown kind of language. We may recognise some of the words people use, words like apostle, prophet and evangelist.[93] But we are not used to hearing these words spoken too often among those sensing a call to lead in the local church. We are in real danger, I believe, in suppressing this move of the Spirit, and of demoralising a generation of leaders, if we do not listen to the way in which that movement is expressed in those coming forward for leadership in the church.

If we truly believe in the gift and divine value of vocation, listening to these voices is listening to the voice of God for what the church must be. We must be willing to take the bold risk of creating space for these vocations to flourish. We must stop forcing people into roles that give insufficient space for their gifts and call to thrive. This will mean tough decisions. It will mean that certain cogs in the ecclesial machine grind to a halt. It will mean investing in risky vocations and in creative individuals who don't quite fit the mould.

But it will, I believe, mean a shift towards shaping the church around its vocational future rather than its past.

Organising in the Spirit therefore means finding new ways of relating with and holding people in accountable relationships, rather than trying to manage them in established structures of roles and responsibilities. It means withholding our tendency towards standard definitions of people and instead seeking to discern what sort of leaders and what kind of ecclesial forms are emerging from the work of the Spirit. Our focus will be primarily on nurturing relationships of encouragement, trust and accountability with leaders, rather than management and control. Furthermore, we will look to further enable the development of this movement by creating the right kind of environment for these leaders and their communities to thrive.

Margaret Wheatley and Deborah Frieze work with leaders of various social movements. They see patterns of development where new leaders emerge from within an established paradigm to found what emerges as the new. They argue that the enabling of these movements requires four key elements:

1 **Naming**: we affirm leaders of such movements by helping people discern and confirm their vocation as a leader within the movement. We also work hard to discern the sorts of leader that the movement is producing, which may be different from those in the more established paradigm.

2 **Networking**: we connect these leaders up in networks, physically and virtually, so that people can gain encouragement and learn from one another.

3 **Nourishing**: we research lessons being learned, patterns of experience and good practice from the movement and then begin to help others with these lessons, so as to enrich and accelerate the movement.

4 **Illuminating**: we shine a light on the new that is starting to take form. Above all, we tell stories that begin to describe the possibilities emerging in areas where the new has until then seemed unimaginable.[94]

Much of this work is highly relational and organic, and it majors in the gift of discernment. Leadership models, patterns of practice and teachable principles emerge from the growing body of experience within the movement. The threat of the dead hand of institutional management must be kept in mind at all times. The loose ties and light supports required at this emergent stage will be primarily relational rather than structural. The new must be given time to reveal its shape before we put a frame on it, lest we impose a frame from our standard store of institutional scaffolding and either kill it or deform it.

Gerald Arbuckle argues, in his discussion of leadership towards a new paradigm of church, that 'the new belongs elsewhere'.[95] I think he is right, but not in the sense that the new must be somehow removed completely from what is considered old. Our own reality of exile is that the old, the new and the indifferent live side-by-side and in close relationship with one another within the broad forms of our structures. However, Arbuckle's arresting phrase does argue for the protected space in which the new can find its identity, its form and to develop enough to have a sustainable future:

A refounding project should not normally be placed in the midst of the existing work/structures, where prophetic people would be under constant critical assessment by members of the community and required to waste invaluable energy 'apologising' for what they are doing.[96]

Any gardener knows that the new requires attention and protection for it to get enough of the light and resources necessary for it to survive to maturity. More established plants will always outcompete seedlings unless there is sufficient space for them to get the resources they need. In terms of the movement towards a new

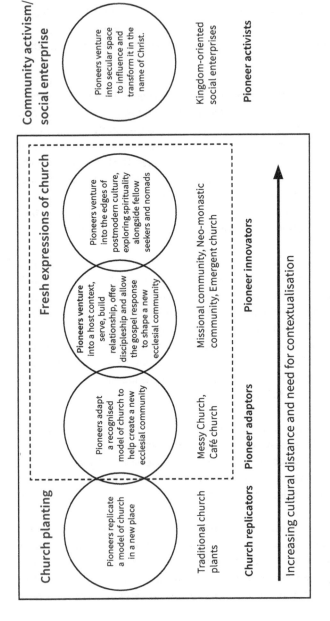

Diagram 1: The pioneer spectrum

paradigm emerging within the old, the tasks of naming, networking, nourishing and illuminating all contribute to providing the kind of protected space in which the new can grow and begin to thrive.

In my work supporting and advocating for pioneers across the south of England, the work of naming has become really important in giving protected space to the kinds of pioneer vocations that are emerging. Conversations with other colleagues, which built on the insights of others, resulted in the 'pioneer spectrum', an attempt to name and describe the range of pioneer vocations we were observing as people came forward for training and support (see Diagram 1 opposite).

This spectrum places different kinds of pioneers on a scale of 'cultural difference', that is, a metaphorical scale of distance in culture from the 'home' culture of church. The spectrum aims to value the vocation of pioneers along the whole spectrum: those planting larger congregational models of church, those innovating often small expressions of church community amid sub-cultures or disconnected communities, and those whose pioneer gift seems to be more expressed in community activism without the intention, at least at the outset, of starting a new church. Each of these vocations is given space on the spectrum and we have found the value that this has conferred on many who have interacted with it really encouraging. It has affirmed the vocations, in particular, of those who feel that the heat and light of large forms of church planting makes their vocation inferior. It has provided a protected space for them to pursue their vocations in their own context with confidence. Crucially, we feel, it has marked out a particular space for innovators, those whose entrepreneurialism is necessary for the life of the whole church, and whose ministry can so easily be disregarded in a church anxious for results and quick returns on its investment.[97]

It strikes me that the exilic literature was one way in which Israel did this work of naming, networking, nourishing and illuminating. This was the way that Israel gave space and time to discern the new that was emerging from the ravages of the old. New kinds of leaders like the priest-prophet Ezekiel and the wise and subversive queen Esther are named in the literature. These leaders create dialogue in the literature, networking with one another as intertextual connections are made. Furthermore, the genre acted to nourish and illuminate the new forms and communities of Jewish life, in Babylon, in Judah and ultimately in the diaspora of Judaism from the exile onwards. It was the way in which Israel harvested the huge amount of innovation – theological, social, ethical, practical – generated by their experience of exile, and then sowed it into the hearts and minds of further generations.

Most significantly, however, is the way in which exile and the response to it gave space for the Spirit to renew Israel. It is the Spirit who takes Ezekiel beyond the edge of the exiled community in order to communicate a vision of a resurrection and renewal beyond the restorationist hopes of the majority. It is the Spirit who creates and then animates the reformation of the bones of a destroyed and discredited army. It is the Spirit who promises to find a space within the people of Israel to bring the new life and bring them home. Exile has created the kind of space beyond the tendency to utilise God, the space in which God can be free to be God in their midst again, the space in which the breath of the Spirit can move once more.

Ezekiel, beyond the place of knowing and the point of surrender, becomes for us a model of participation in the life of the Spirit. He becomes a model of how someone, schooled in the establishment, can respond to a new context and curate the kind of space in which the Spirit of resurrection and renewal can work. He becomes a model of the kind of charismatic leader who knows how to participate in the work of the Spirit, leading from the edge more than the front, allowing the new to emerge and unfold, stage by stage. He becomes a model of the exilic leader who refuses to entertain the soothing image of restoration or a master plan of the future, but instead urges the church into a new participative relationship with the Spirit. For the new paradigm, the new home for the people of God, both for Ezekiel in his exile or for us in ours, will be discovered by following a different route. In particular, it will not come from above but 'from below'. It will come when the church, with the encouragement and humility of discerning leaders, takes up the invitation to participate in the Spirit's leading towards a refounded church.

Notes

1   Walter Brueggemann, *Cadences of Home* (John Knox, 1997), p. 2.
2   Lee Beach, *The Church in Exile* (IVP, 2015), p. 36.
3   Alan Roxburgh, *The Missionary Congregation, Leadership and Liminality* (Trinity Press, 1997), p. 13.
4   Daniel Smith-Christopher, *A Biblical Theology of Exile* (Augsburg Fortress, 2002), p. 59.
5   Smith-Christopher, *A Biblical Theology of Exile*, p. 47.
6   Smith-Christopher, *A Biblical Theology of Exile*, p. 48.
7   Daniel Smith-Christopher, *The Religion of the Landless* (Wipf and Stock, 1989), pp. 117–18.
8   Smith-Christopher, *A Biblical Theology of Exile*, p. 73.
9   Brueggemann, *Cadences of Home*, p. 3.
10 Paul Bradbury, *Stepping into Grace* (BRF, 2016), p. 63.
11 See Eugene Peterson, *Five Smooth Stones for Pastoral Work* (Eerdmans, 1980), chapter 3.
12 E.V. Daniel and J.C. Knudsen quoted in Smith-Christopher, *A Biblical Theology of Exile*, p. 80.
13 Sam Wells, *A Future that's Bigger than the Past*, Renewal and Reform Background Paper (2016), **churchofengland.org/about/renewal-and-reform/more-about-renewal-reform/theological-reflections**.
14 Brueggemann, *Cadences of Home*, p. 1.
15 Quoted in Beach, *The Church in Exile*, p. 19.
16 Beach, *The Church in Exile*, p. 46.
17 Christopher J.H. Wright, *The Message of Ezekiel* (IVP, 2001), p. 26.
18 Wright, *The Message of Ezekiel*, p. 26.
19 Jonny Baker, **jonnybaker.blogs.com/jonnybaker/2008/11/the-gift-of-not.html**.
20 Walter Brueggemann, *Hopeful Imagination* (Fortress, 1986), p. 59.
21 Gerald Arbuckle, *Refounding the Church* (Geoffrey Chapman, 1993), p. 113.
22 '*Walk Outs* are people who bravely choose to leave behind a world of unsolvable problems, scarce resources, limiting beliefs and destructive individualism. They *walk on* to the ideas, beliefs and practices that enable them to give birth to new systems that serve

community.' See **walkoutwalkon.net** and the work of Margaret Wheatley and Deborah Frieze.

23 A phrase used by the organisation Art of Hosting. 'At the edge of chaos is where life innovates – where things are not hard wired, but are flexible enough for new connections and solutions to occur. New levels of order become possible out of chaos.' See **artofhosting.org/ the-chaordic-path**.

24 Brueggemann, *Cadences of Home*, p. 109.

25 For a fuller exploration of the lament form, see Paul Bradbury, *Sowing in Tears* (Grove, 2007), chapter 3.

26 Brueggemann, *Cadences of Home*, p. 17.

27 Brueggemann, *Cadences of Home*, p. 4.

28 Brueggemann, *Cadences of Home*, p. 4.

29 Beach, *The Church in Exile*, p. 144.

30 A story I personally heard Bishop Graham Cray tell.

31 This is the Mission Shaped Ministry course, **missionshapedministry. org**, which can be run as a conventional course, or in a more flexible way that enables trainers to tailor the material to the team's needs and context.

32 See, for example, Ezekiel 8:6, 12, 17; 12:9, 22; 15:2; 20:4.

33 These stories can be found in 1 Kings 17:17–24; 2 Kings 4:18–37; and 2 Kings 13:20–21.

34 See Gerald May, *The Dark Night of the Soul* (Harper Collins, 2005), chapter 1.

35 May, *The Dark Night of the Soul*, p. 67.

36 Walter Brueggemann, *Hopeful Imagination* (Fortress Press, 1986), p. 1.

37 Brueggemann, *Hopeful Imagination*, p. 3.

38 Barbara Brown Taylor, *Learning to Walk in the Dark* (Canterbury Press, 2014), p. 141.

39 Tom Stuckey, *Singing the Lord's Song in a Strange Land* (Church in the Market Place, 2017), p. 103.

40 Brueggemann, *Hopeful Imagination*, p. 55.

41 May, *The Dark Night of the Soul*, p. 92.

42 Eugene Peterson, *The Contemplative Pastor* (Eerdmans, 1989), chapter 9.

43 David Runcorn, *The Road to Growth Less Travelled* (Grove, 2008), p. 17.

44 Steve Addison, *Movements that Changed the World* (IVP, 2009), pp. 87–92.

45 Brueggemann, *Hopeful Imagination*, p. 63.

46 Brueggemann, *Hopeful Imagination*, p. 71.

47 See **cofepioneer.org/pioneermeaning**.

48 See, for example, Dave Male, *How to Pioneer (Even if you haven't a clue)* (SCM, 2016), which is a highly accessible and hugely helpful introduction to pioneering.

49 Wright, *The Message of Ezekiel*, p. 310.

50 Ralph W. Klein, *Israel in Exile* (Fortress, 1979), p. 84.

51 John V. Taylor, *The Go-Between God* (SCM, 2004), p. 120.

52 See, for example, Beth Keith, *Authentic Faith: Fresh expressions of church amongst young adults* (Fresh Expressions, 2013).

53 Brueggemann, *Hopeful Imagination*, p. 79.

54 Taylor, *The Go-Between God*, p. 126.

55 Taylor, *The Go-Between God*, p. 148.

56 Taylor, *The Go-Between God*, p. 149.

57 Robert Colville, *The Great Acceleration: How the world is getting faster, faster* (Bloomsbury, 2016).

58 **lifeathome.ikea.com/explore/static/press/IKEA_Life_At_Home_Report_3.pdf**

59 **lifeathome.ikea.com/explore/static/press/IKEA_Life_At_Home_Report_3.pdf**, p. 7.

60 Brueggemann, *Hopeful Imagination*, p. 66.

61 T.S. Eliot, 'The Journey of the Magi', in *Collected Poems 1909–1962* (Faber and Faber Ltd, 2017). Used by permission.

62 **poetryarchive.org/guided-tour/tour-archive-dr-rowan-williams**

63 Beach, *The Church in Exile*, p. 59.

64 Brueggemann, *Hopeful Imagination*, p. 55.

65 The concept of *missio Dei* was developed in particular by David Bosch: see *Transforming Mission* (Orbis, 2007), p. 390.

66 Hugh McCleod quoted in Stefan Paas, *Church Planting in the Secular West* (Eerdman, 2016), p. 58.

67 Alan Hirsch, *The Forgotten Ways* (Brazos Press, 2006), p. 30.

68 Daniel Smith-Christopher, *The Religion of the Landless* (Wipf & Stock, 1989), chapter 6.

69 Smith-Christopher, *The Religion of the Landless*, p. 148.

70 Brueggemann, *Cadences of Home*, p. 9.

71 Brueggemann, *Cadences of Home*, p. 8.

72 Kenneth Bailey, *Jacob and the Prodigal* (IVP, 2003).

73 **reconnect-poole.org.uk/wp-content/uploads/2017/07/Ruleoflife.pdf**

74 Walter Brueggemann, *Sabbath as Resistance* (Westminster John Knox, 2014), p. 88.

75   Brueggemann, *Cadences of Home*, p. 6.

76   Allen Mailer, quoted in Beach, *The Church in Exile*, p. 63.

77   Lesslie Newbigin, *The Gospel in a Pluralist Society* (Eerdmans, 1989), p. 227.

78   W. Lee Humphreys quoted in Smith-Christopher, *The Religion of the Landless*, p. 160.

79   Rowan Williams, *Silence and Honey Cakes*, chapter 1.

80   billygrahamlibrary.org/crusade-city-spotlight-london

81   billygrahamlibrary.org/crusade-city-spotlight-london

82   Graham Cray, *Discerning Leadership* (Grove, 2010).

83   Rowan Williams, *Being Disciples* (SPCK, 2016), p. 4.

84   Lesslie Newbigin quoted in Cray, *Discerning Leadership*, p. 7.

85   Graham Tomlin, *The Widening Circle* (SPCK, 2014), pp. 113–14.

86   Jürgen Moltmann in Jane Williams (ed.), *The Holy Spirit in the World Today* (Alpha International, 2001), p. 18.

87   Jürgen Moltmann in Williams, *The Holy Spirit in the World Today*, p. 26.

88   Phyllis Tickle, *The Great Emergence* (Baker Books, 2012), p. 51.

89   Harvey Cox, *The Future of Faith* (HarperCollins, 2009).

90   **ampltd.co.uk/digital_guides/church_missionary_society_archive_ general/editorial%20introduction%20by%20rosemary%20keen. aspx**

91   **pioneer.churchmissionsociety.org**

92   churchtimes.co.uk/articles/2010/26-november/books-arts/book-reviews/the-baby-and-the-parochial-bathwater

93   Alan Hirsch has argued in a number of publications that the Christendom model of church modelled its leaders on the pastor-teacher and paid little attention to apostles, prophets and evangelists, the other three dimensions of the five-fold ministry description of the church in Ephesians 4. He argues that a new missional context urges the church to rediscover and re-emphasise these neglected gifts in its leadership. See *The Shaping of Things to Come* (Hendrickson, 2003), chapter 10; *The Permanent Revolution* (Jossey Bass, 2012); *5Q* (100 Movements, 2017).

94   Margaret Wheatley and Deborah Frieze, *Walk Out Walk On* (Berrett-Koehler, 2011), p. 226.

95   Arbuckle, *Refounding the Church*, p. 119.

96   Arbuckle, *Refounding the Church*, p. 151.

97   churchmissionsociety.org/resources/pioneering-mission-spectrum-tina-hodgett-paul-bradbury-anvil-vol-34-issue-1

Stepping into Grace finds powerful connections between the call and mission of Jonah and the mission context of our own time. Using the narrative thread of the biblical story to explore themes of ambition, vocation, spirituality, mission, leadership and personal growth, it argues for a ministry rooted in grace, where who we are becoming in Christ provides a foundation for our participation in the mission of God. This unique journey takes us to a place of grace where the work of God, in shaping who we are, finds space alongside what we feel called to do.

Stepping into Grace
Moving beyond ambition to contemplative mission
Paul Bradbury
978 0 85746 523 8 £7.99

brfonline.org.uk

'A written masterclass' Paul Wilcox

You
are more
important
than your MINISTRY

SUSTAINING LEADERSHIP

PAUL SWANN

Many books on leadership and ministry are written from the point of view of success and strength. In *Sustaining Leadership*, Paul Swann writes out of the raw experience of failure, getting to the heart of who we are as leaders rather than what we do. From this, he offers both hope and practical resources for sustaining effective long-term ministry, looking at self-care, balance and healthy ministry, feasting on divine love, and more. As he says, this is the best gift we can offer those we serve.

Sustaining Leadership
You are more important than your ministry
Paul Swann
978 0 85746 651 8 £8.99

brfonline.org.uk

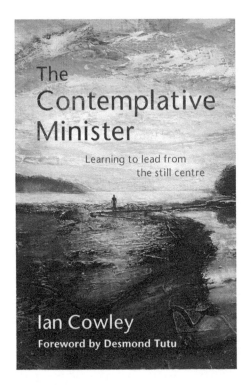

Ian Cowley offers direction for contemplative leaders in the 21st century, drawing on his South African roots and the influence of contemplative leaders such as Desmond Tutu. He explains practically how to prioritise a relationship with God and lead others into that relationship, creating a shared ministry to allow the leader to nurture faith and spirituality amid the hectic life that is ministry today.

The Contemplative Minister
Learning to lead from the still centre
Ian Cowley
978 0 85746 360 9 £8.99

brfonline.org.uk

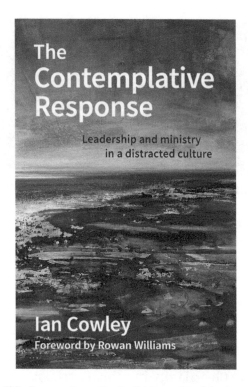

The true self finds peace in resting in the love of God, in the peace which Jesus promises. Jesus says to each of us in ministry, 'As the Father has loved me, so have I loved you. Abide, rest, dwell, in my love' (John 15:9). This book will seek to show what this might mean for those in Christian ministry in the 21st century.

The Contemplative Response
Leadership and ministry in a distracted culture
Ian Cowley
978 0 85746 656 3 £8.99

brfonline.org.uk

Transforming
lives and communities

Christian growth and understanding of the Bible

Resourcing individuals, groups and leaders in churches for their own spiritual journey and for their ministry

Church outreach in the local community

Offering two programmes that churches are embracing to great effect as they seek to engage with their local communities and transform lives

The Gift of Years

Teaching Christianity in primary schools

Working with children and teachers to explore Christianity creatively and confidently

Children's and family ministry

Working with churches and families to explore Christianity creatively and bring the Bible alive

parenting for faith

Visit **brf.org.uk** for more information on BRF's work

brf.org.uk

The Bible Reading Fellowship (BRF) is a Registered Charity (No. 233280)